THE 8 CAREER SKILLS YOU DIDN'T LEARN IN COLLEGE

BY SAM OWENS

ISBN: 978-1-70-587917-7

PRAISE FOR *THE 8 CAREER SKILLS YOU DIDN'T LEARN IN COLLEGE*.

For anyone wanting to ease the rocky transition between the academic world and the corporate one, this superb book does the job! Filled with powerful advice along with essential "how-to's," Sam Owens delivers both wonderful insight and practical application. He generously shares his wisdom (and his mistakes) openly with the reader in an easy-to-follow format as he provides an illuminating path to follow. The perfect graduation gift!

— Stephen M. R. Covey, *The New York Times* & #1 *Wall Street Journal* bestselling author of *The Speed of Trust*

Having worked with employees at all levels over the last thirty years, I can say that these 8 career skills are what really matter in the end. Told in a fun, easy to understand, and engaging way, Sam has figured out how to articulate the "squishy" part of business. I wish I had read this book when I was starting out. It would have helped me avoid a lot of mistakes.

— Doug Behrens, President and CCO Kind Snacks

The Corporate Career Textbook is a fantastic reference for anyone looking to bridge the wide chasm between classroom learning and real-world doing.

— Kerry Patterson, *The New York Times* bestselling author of *Crucial Conversations*

An excellent depiction of what to really expect when stepping into the business world. Not surprisingly, there is a lot more to it than what you learn in school. Sam provides navigation on how to prepare for the ambiguity that lies ahead. This is a must read for any undergrad or MBA student or someone already in their career.

— Bob Tansil, Vice President and Corporate Recruiter, O'Connell Group

College doesn't get you a successful career anymore, the skills in this book do. Sam fills in the cracks on principles we should all know, many of which I'm still learning.

— Travis Chambers, Founder and CEO of Chamber.Media and Forbes 30 under 30 Entrepreneur

Armed with the skills laid out in this book, young professionals can skip five years of mistakes and start winning at work immediately.

— Jodi Glickman, CEO and Founder, Great on the Job

" *Sam* makes principles of real-world success accessible through the use of entertaining and relatable stories. Each chapter presents a framework for a different career skill which can both improve your own performance and help those you mentor.

— Jacob Thomas, Senior Director,
Union Pacific Railroad

" *I'm* convinced that if young professionals apply these 8 principles, they'll quickly separate themselves at work and accelerate their careers.

— Tim Nangle, Vice President and General Manager,
ConAgra Brands

CONTENTS

Author's Note: Throughout this book, I use the pronoun "he" instead of "she" or "he or she." I do this not for exclusivity, but for simplicity. The content of this book applies to both men and women.

INTRODUCTION

I N APRIL OF 2009, I SAT IN THE FINAL CLASS OF MY LAST SEMES-
ter of business school. The global economy at that time was
in the midst of the worst economic downturn since the Great
Depression. Just one month before, the Dow Jones Industrial
Average Index had fallen below 7,000 points, down over fifty
percent from the prior year! Economists predicted that, unlike prior recessions that had seen speedy recoveries, this re-
cession would be deep, slow, and painful. Corporations were
hoarding cash and implementing hiring freezes. Mass layoffs
across the country had already started. Everyone looking for
a job at that time felt the reverberating effects of the reces-
sion and MBA students looking for jobs were feeling the pinch.
During normal economic times, nine out of ten students at my
school could count on having a good job lined up at graduation.
But in April 2009, just two weeks before graduation, only five
out of ten of my classmates had secured employment offers.
Furthermore, in order to get these offers, many of them had
abandoned their dreams of switching careers and went back to

the same positions they had held before business school. Others took jobs with little or no pay just to get a good company name on their resumes to leverage when the economy picked up again. Uncertainty, frustration, and anxiety were palpable throughout the school halls that spring.

It was against this backdrop that my finance professor stood before his class of twenty or so students to give his final lecture. This ninety minutes would be different from his other lectures. Unlike the other classes we had attended that semester, this one had no subject listed on the syllabus. There was no requirement to read a case study prior to class; no papers, analysis, or spreadsheets to turn in. Rather, he had reserved this time solely for the purpose of telling his students what he felt would benefit them the most in the years ahead. Given the economic environment at the time, he knew his students would be listening very carefully.

This professor was not your typical academic. He had not spent his career teaching, publishing research, or writing textbooks. He did not have a PhD, and corrected anyone who addressed him as "Dr." (he did, however, have a Master of Business Administration degree, and jokingly requested that we use the prefix "Master.") He had spent his career as a partner of the prestigious investment bank, Goldman Sachs. The university had brought him on board three years prior to leverage his vast network of business contacts and to help share with students how things work outside of academia. Anything he may have lacked in complex academic theory or classroom etiquette he more than compensated for with financial expertise, real-world experience, and an innate feel for how things actually got done at major corporations.

There was an uncomfortable silence in the room that day. It was almost as if every student had personally asked him in desperation for his best advice and he was preparing to give it to all of us at once. His demeanor showed the weight of the obligation that he felt to each of us. Deep down, he knew that many of his students would struggle for a couple of years before finding the right job—or any job at all. In a paltry hour and a half, he hoped to say something that would minimize that struggle. Despite this daunting task, he maintained an optimistic and even cheerful demeanor. He knew his students could use all the encouragement they could get.

What would he say? I suspect some of us were hoping for a new angle; perhaps a new technique or model we could apply to separate ourselves from the competition. Others, especially the "straight A" types, wanted to hear that good grades in the past would ensure success in the future; that there was a direct correlation between high marks in business school and worldly prosperity afterward. After all, we were all accustomed to the U.S. educational system using grades to tell us whether or not we were worth anything. Want to go to a good college? Get good grades in high school. Want to go to a good graduate school? Get good grades in college. Even in elementary and middle schools, it was grades that teachers, parents, and peers used to assess one's potential in this world. Why should it be any different after school?

Finally, I suppose there were those who wanted to hear about good old-fashioned hard work, ethics, determination, and the like. We liked the notion that anyone can be wildly successful, provided he is willing to work harder than the next person. To believe otherwise would almost be un-American! We had all read stories of people who came from nothing but worked day and night to eventually achieve their dreams. Success through hard work was part of the cultural fabric woven into our educational lives from a young age.

What he told us, however, was something different entirely. I will never forget his opening statement. "I wish we offered a class here on schmoozing," he said. Then he went on to explain that the most important skills needed to succeed in a corporation had not been taught to us in the previous two years. Everything we had learned in our coursework, from financial modeling to strategic thinking to how to survive on three hours of sleep was good—even necessary. Those things would all be part of wearing the corporate uniform, yet they alone would never determine whether or not we would win the game. According to him, winning required more than hard work, integrity, and smarts; more than what a finance test or bar exam or medical board exam could measure. Success, he said, would require a different set of skills. This included knowing how to sell yourself without coming off as arrogant, when to speak up and when to shut up in a meeting, the appropriate time to give your boss some bad news, how to get people excited about boring topics, how to turn data into a riveting story, how to create a vision that is simple enough for an entire team to grasp, and much, much more.

To be successful over the course of our business careers, we would need *corporate* skills, not classroom skills.

I left class that day underwhelmed and disappointed. I had invested two years of my life in higher education, foregone a good salary from a decent paying job, gone into debt, cooped up my wife and two children in an apartment with forest green carpet and terrible lighting, and the golden nugget of final wisdom was corporate skills? Schmoozing? What? I felt like I was a character in *The Wizard of Oz* who had traveled to the Emerald City of education with Dorothy, the Lion, the Scarecrow, and the Tin Man to hear the secrets that would grant them their innermost desires (a way home, courage, a brain, a heart, and, in my case, a successful career at a high-profile corporation). Instead, I had discovered a little old man behind a curtain with nothing useful to say. Surely my tuition and time deserved more than this!

Three months later, I found myself in the thick of corporate life (I was one of the lucky ones to actually *have* a job) and quickly realized that my judgment of the professor's advice had been dead wrong. Not only was his advice the best I had received in business school, but it was the best career advice I had received—ever.

I had the benefit of watching a perfectly structured case study of the power of corporate skills in my first three years of employment. It involved two employees, whom I'll call Jared and Lee. These newly-hired individuals had, on the surface, nearly everything in common. They had been hired at the same time and they had very impressive resumes. They came directly from prominent business schools. Each had a healthy combination of brains and ambition. Had you been the person to interview these candidates for the position, you would have had a tough time guessing which candidate would perform better at the company. They both seemed to have very bright corporate futures.

Within the first couple of months, Lee began to confide in me that he wasn't enjoying his job. His boss always seemed frustrated with him and he didn't understand why. Oddly, there wasn't one specific problem that he could point to. The actual work wasn't overly hard for him. He understood how to complete each of his core tasks. He was working hard, yet something still wasn't clicking. He was not being pulled into meetings to help make decisions on his business. His boss would often exclude him from important conversations, saying that she had forgotten or that she wanted him to use his time completing other assignments. After a few more months, the company had him reporting to someone else, thinking that perhaps his personality just wasn't a good fit with that of his manager's. Yet the problems persisted. Finally, he was put on a formal Performance Improvement Plan, which in many companies is a coded message that means, "Go find another job before we fire you." Within a little over a year, Lee left the company.

Jared, on the other hand, hit the ground running. He, like Lee, was working hard and felt he understood his tasks. But unlike Lee, he *was* being pulled into important meetings. His manager included him in important decisions and seemed to delight in mentoring and training him. What's more, Jared seemed to know everyone on his floor within the first three months. Even though the workload got tedious at times, he always felt like people were behind him. After his first year on the job, Jared was promoted.

While this example may be dramatic (most new employees aren't either promoted or fired after a year), it is a powerful example of the broader reality in business organizations: People of seemingly equal qualifications succeed or fail over time based on factors that are subjective and difficult to measure.

Warren Buffett, the legendary billionaire investor and CEO of Berkshire Hathaway, one of the largest corporations in the world, described this reality in 2007 to a group of students at the University of Florida:

> Think for a moment that I granted you the right to buy ten percent in one of your classmates for the rest of his or her lifetime...who are you going to invest in? Are you going to pick the one with the highest IQ? I doubt it. Are you going to pick the one with the most energy? Probably not. Are you are going to pick the one with the best grades? I doubt it. Are you going to pick the most energetic? Are you going to pick the one who displays the most initiative?
>
> No, you are going to look for more qualitative factors. I would say that if you thought about it, you'd pick the one you responded the best to; the one that was going to have the leadership qualities; the one that was going to be able to get other people to carry out their interests.

Then Buffett went on to describe the opposite scenario:

> Now let's say you wanted to go short [meaning, bet against the success of] another person in the class. Again, you wouldn't pick the person with the lowest IQ. You would start to think about the person who really turned you off for one reason or another... you just didn't want to be around them and other people didn't want to be around them.

Central to Buffett's message is that "qualitative factors," not IQ, can cause a person not only to break through to incredible success, but also to fail miserably. According to Buffett, it's not all about smarts, grades, or correct classroom answers. Many times, it's not even about results (just look how long politicians are allowed to stay in office!). It's about a set of qualities and behaviors that are difficult to measure but real nonetheless.

These qualities are critical to succeed not only in large corporations, but in non-profit organizations, churches, governments, small enterprises, and every other formally organized entity. To illustrate this principle, I will use an example in the medical field. My wife, Gina, and I have four children. Each child was born in a different U.S. state. Each was delivered by a different doctor. As she looks back, Gina has different and somewhat strong opinions about each doctor. She loved two of the doctors. One of them she thought was OK. One of them she strongly disliked.

I had a front-row seat throughout this process. I carefully observed each doctor's approach toward Gina. By what criteria do you think she measured each doctor's success in treating her? Was it the technical skill with which our children were delivered? No. Each child came out OK and is still healthy. What about the doctor's educational background? Nope. Gina never even asked where they went to school, nor did she care. How about experience? No again. It was never a topic of conversation.

So what was it, then?

When Gina and I talked about the doctor she didn't like, she would say things like "He didn't listen to anything I said," or "I felt like he cared more about just getting the baby delivered than actually caring for me," or "He wanted to get the baby out so he could collect his check and go home and go to bed." I observed the same thing about this doctor. He may have been a great doctor, technically speaking, but he had some traits that rubbed us the wrong way.

Now listen to her comments about one of the doctors she loved to work with. "He was so sweet during my delivery. While the nurses were getting impatient waiting for the baby to come, he was calm, steady and encouraging the whole time. He just kept saying 'I know she can do this, she just needs a little more time.'"

Here are her comments about the other doctor she liked: "I saw the doctor today for my routine check-up. I think I'm one of his favorite patients! He gave me a big hug and was so sweet to our little Charlotte. I'm so sad he's retiring. Do you think he'd be willing to come out of retirement just for me to deliver our next baby?"

Throughout these observations of and conversations with Gina, it became clear that the doctors' educational backgrounds had no bearing on which doctor she would choose to see again. Granted, medical school made these people doctors. But what made these people *great* doctors was not medical school. It was a set of skills that they developed over time. These included the ability to make a patient feel important, the ability to influence and persuade a patient toward the proper treatment, and the ability to keep a patient's family comfortable during the whole process. These skills are likely not listed on these doctors' resumes, but they make all the difference. Patients vote with their wallets. A doctor's impeccable education cannot compensate for patients who don't like him.

The example of these four doctors is at the very core of my finance professor's message that March of 2009. You win in the classroom by using classroom skills; you win in a corporation by using corporate skills. He did not give us advice on how to develop these skills—he left that up to us. His message was one of warning: if we wanted to understand how to win in the corporate environment, we needed to figure out the true rules of the game and learn to play by them. Not to do so would surely be damaging to our careers.

Since that last finance class eight years ago, I've worked with hundreds of people who wrestle with career challenges. Some of these people are dealing with such difficult bosses that their daily work is miserable. Others are being told they aren't good "fits" in their organizations, a message they don't know how to interpret. Many are doing very well at their companies but are considering quitting because they believe they can progress faster somewhere else. Some feel like they are being underpaid and don't know how to approach getting a raise. Others are first-time bosses and are completely overwhelmed by being responsible for others. Others have a big presentation coming up and don't know how to start preparing. These are real challenges with major career implications. A college education does basically nothing to help solve them.

Personally, I've learned how to navigate these issues not with academic knowledge, but through years of on-the-job trial and error. In some cases, I've been able to help solve co-workers' challenges by serving as a mentor and teacher. In other cases, I've benefited from the mentorship of others whose experience far outweighed my own. It's been through tangible—

and sometimes painful—experience that I've figured out how to approach these problems.

To spare you the learning curve I experienced, I have developed a skill-based framework to help you succeed in the corporate world. I use the word "skill" deliberately and emphatically. These are not motivational anecdotes. They are not new mindsets or quick tips. They are learnable, practical skills that can be mastered through dedicated attention and practice. If you ignore these skills, you will someday find yourself stagnant and unhappy in your job. But if you learn and apply them, they will propel you past your peers for years to come.

Here are the eight corporate skills you didn't learn in college.

1

COMPANY 101–THE CORPORATION VERSUS THE CLASSROOM

Toto, I have a feeling we're not in Kansas anymore.
—The Wonderful Wizard of Oz

The Appeal of a Corporate Career

I F YOUR CAREER FOLLOWS THE SAME TREND AS THE AVERAGE U.S. worker, you will spend about forty years of your life in full-time employment. Assuming a forty-five-hour work week and three weeks of vacation per year, you will spend a total of 88,200 hours working. To put this into context, for those forty years, you will spend approximately forty percent of your waking hours working—fifty percent if you exclude weekends. That's likely more time then you'll spend with your spouse, with your children, exercising and pursuing hobbies—combined. It's a little sad, really. Needless to say, finding a fulfilling and enjoyable career should be regarded as one of the most important decisions you'll ever make.

Some people decide to be doctors, dentists, teachers, or trade workers. Others choose public service or small business ownership. Still others choose to be artists or musicians. And, yes, a good chunk of people choose to place their bets on a corporate career. If you are reading this book, this has likely been your choice—and what a fantastic choice it is! A corporate career can be exciting, intellectually stimulating, profitable, and fulfilling. It can provide the stability that will set you and your family up for long-term financial security. It can provide a structure and routine to help you achieve a reasonable level of balance in your life. It can allow you to build long-lasting relationships and grow your capacity to influence others.

Many new college graduates get the "entrepreneurial itch," preferring to skip a corporate job in favor of starting a business immediately after they graduate. After all, most of the world's richest people did that very same thing, right? Wrong. In fact, the vast majority of the world's most successful entrepreneurs started their careers working for someone else at a corporation—Jeff Bezos of Amazon.com, Larry Ellison of Oracle, Jim Sinegal of Costco Wholesale, and Warren Buffet of Berkshire Hathaway, to name a few. Their time working for a large company provided them with the foundational experience and personal contacts to venture out on their own. Many got their big ideas by seeing a specific need that was not being met in their industries. Even if you were born to be an entrepreneur, earning your stripes at a big company can only help you in the long run.

I recognize that working for yourself sounds prestigious, but what is prestigious about doing your own billing and collections, paying fully for your health insurance, and being your own IT department? When you work for a corporation and your computer decides to burn out, guess what? You make one phone call and a new computer is delivered to your desk free of charge, usually accompanied by a person willing to help you get it set up! What if you aren't feeling well one week? When you run your own business, your customers don't care how you feel. Corporations, on the other hand, have built-in policies for sick leave, with no adverse effects on your current pay or long-term career. And what about collecting payments from customers? At a big company, unless you work in accounts payable, you'll never have to collect a bill in your life.

And let's not forget the financial value of corporate benefits. These benefits, including health insurance, retirement plans, paid vacation, and other perks are worth approximately thirty percent of an employee's salary[1]. So, if you are a corporate employee making $60,000 per year and are considering starting your own business, you'd have to make nearly $80,000 in *take-home profit* (don't mistake profit for sales) per year on your own to make up for all the other perks that you will be giving up. And that doesn't account for the instability and ambiguity created when you go out on your own.

As an entrepreneur, your chances of failure are very high. The U.S. Department of Labor tracks the survival rate of new ventures. One study, released in 2015, shows the fate of new businesses since 1994. The trends are remarkably consistent. After three years, businesses have nearly a forty percent chance

---

1   Bureau of Labor Statistics *Employer Costs for Employee Compensation Survey—September 2016.*

of failing. After ten years, failure rates are in the sixty-five percent range. What if you want to start a business and work it for
your entire forty-year career? Well, the survey doesn't have
forty years of historical data to predict your chances. But it
does have twenty-two years of data and, of those businesses
started in 1994, less than twenty percent are left!

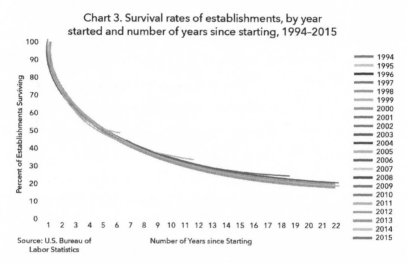

Chart 3. Survival rates of establishments, by year
started and number of years since starting, 1994–2015

Note: these lines are easier to read in full color, but you get
the idea: regardless of the year a business started, the odds
of failure were about the same.

Don't get me wrong, you can get rich—really, really rich—
by being an entrepreneur. The richest entrepreneurs, as a
general rule, have more money than the richest corporate
executives. And it is true that if you own your own company,
you technically won't have a boss. But don't think that working for yourself means that you answer *only* to yourself. Customers often can be worse taskmasters than bosses. Bosses
are incentivized to help you succeed; customers care solely
about results.

Granted, working for a corporation has its hassles (many of which I'll address shortly), but a corporate job can be very attractive—especially when you are starting your career. Here are some things a corporation can get you as you enter the workforce:

Money: Corporations are willing to pay you more than you are worth for a period after they hire you. This is because they have a current base of paying customers that gives them leverage to invest in the future value you will bring into the company. Entrepreneurs, on the other hand, begin with zero customers. Starting out, you won't make a dime until a prospective customer thinks you're worth it.

Training: Many companies have formal training programs to build your skills. You will also learn a lot about how an industry works through on-the-job training. You'll get valuable on-the-job training as an entrepreneur as well. The difference is that, at a big company, you will be learning the hard lessons with someone else's money.

Scale: You will likely be given way more responsibility than you deserve when you work for a big company. For example, I currently manage a business that does $600 million in revenue annually. I have a multi-million dollar marketing budget and I lead various teams in different departments on large-scale projects. Dozens of people built that business over decades before giving it to me.

Street Cred: Whether you deserve it or not, a few years with a big company will give you an attractive resume. This helps if you ever decide to leave. If you make the jump to a smaller company, you'll be able to leverage your resume to get more money and more responsibility at your new employer. Or, if you want to go out on your own, your credibility can get you customers and investors.

Perks: I mentioned health insurance and retirement plans earlier in this chapter, but I was just scratching the surface. There are so many additional perks a company can offer you, including tuition reimbursement, relocation services, free gym memberships, and a subsidized cafeteria. When you have to travel, you can do it in style with a corporate credit card. When you travel as an entrepreneur, you may be sleeping on a relative's couch.

Contacts: A big company can help you build your personal network of experts. Since industries tend to be micro-communities—everyone knows everyone—these contacts can help you get jobs in the future. Or, if you have a great business idea but not all the expertise, you'll know who to call.

I don't list all of these advantages of a corporate career to talk you out of being an entrepreneur. Indeed, if you are meant to be an entrepreneur, the arguments I've laid out have likely not dissuaded you anyway. I make these points only to assert the notion that, if you aren't sure whether or not to work for a big company or own your own business, you do yourself no harm by getting some corporate experience first. Whether you like it and choose to stay, or hate it and choose to leave, it is a great place to build the foundation for your career.

The Corporate Mindset

Despite all its advantages, a corporate career can be a miserable failure for a lot of people. Some find it extremely frustrating and draining. Many give up and leave—or are asked to leave—the corporate life long before it starts to get really fun and lucrative (the words "fun" and "lucrative" so often accompany one another!). Some stick around but underperform their potential. Others succeed financially but still remain exhausted and unhappy despite the money they are making.

The primary reason people get frustrated with corporate life is that they enter it with unrealistic expectations. For many new corporate employees, there is a gap between what they expect a corporate job to be like and what it is really like. Many expect it to be less work. Others think their individual talents should be more valued. Some are thrown off by office politics. Many think they should have more flexibility in their schedules. The whole experience can be very disillusioning.

Naturally, no one completely knows what he is getting into until he actually experiences it. Some people, however, enter a corporation with more distorted views than the rest. These are the people who don't make it.

The birthplace of these unrealistic expectations is the classroom. High school and college are terrible models for how things work in the real world. The classroom is where you learn about things in conceptual terms and don't worry about how things actually get done. It is where you learn behaviors that don't translate into the workplace, like complaining to your teacher about your grade or expecting to get showered with praise for doing what is asked of you. The very behaviors that help you get ahead in college will often punish you in the workplace. In fact, the entire mindset that leads to success in the classroom is fundamentally different from the mindset that will lead to success at a corporation. Let me lay out a few examples of how the classroom mindset is different from the corporate mindset. The quicker you can adapt to the corporate mindset, the more successful you will be in your job.

Classroom Mindset: *Good grades in school will result in a successful career for me.*

Corporate Mindset: *Your grades may have helped me get your job, but they will have no bearing on whether or not you will keep it. Go ahead and toss your transcripts in the garbage, because nobody cares anymore. Your parents and professors may have well patted you on the back for your 4.0 GPA, but don't tell your work friends about that unless you want them to think you are immature and smug. Leave your grades back in school where they belong.*

Classroom Mindset: *I am naturally smart, so I will excel at my job.*

Corporate Mindset: *Welcome to the business world, where there are hundreds of thousands of people just as smart as you. They also tested well on standardized tests and didn't have to study much in college.*

Classroom Mindset: *But I'm not just smart, I'm really, really smart.*

Corporate Mindset: *In that case, your situation is riskier than that of a half-wit. You run the risk of being "indispensable," which is business-speak for "You are the only one smart enough to be in this role, so we can't promote you and give you other experiences because we need you here." Without the right tools, you will have to fight against getting pigeon-holed for your career into a job that you don't want.*

Think twice before letting people know you are brilliant or have specialized talent.

Classroom Mindset: *I will succeed because I will work harder than anyone else*

Corporate Mindset: *You probably don't work harder than anyone else. If you do, then your life is out of balance, because there are millions of people out there who are willing to make work their #1 priority. Ironically, many of the hardest-working people are not the ones that get promoted. They generally have some sort of other deficiency and they are trying to compensate for it. They think that if they only work harder—put in more hours—that somehow their other glaring weaknesses will go away. Corporations will keep these people around because they do a lot of the work, but they don't necessarily want to promote them. Hard work doesn't earn any extra credit at large corporations. They expect hard work and they're not surprised when someone decides to put in extra hours. What's more, if you decide to put in some extra hours to get ahead in the short term, you are setting a negative precedent that may turn into a future expectation. Be careful about working harder than you can sustain over the long term; your boss may grow accustomed to it.*

Classroom Mindset: *I really don't need my manager hovering over me all the time. He acts like my coach but the reality is I'm smarter than he is. I did fine in school without a manager and I will do fine at work without one as well. I just don't think having something telling me what to do all the time is productive.*

Corporate Mindset: *Making your manager happy is a part of corporate life. You may think you are smarter than* *him and that you don't need him, but you do. Throughout your career, you will have managers that you like and managers you don't like, and you will have to figure out a way to keep them happy. Why? Because they are the single most important factor in your career progression and your daily happiness.*

Classroom Mindset: *Most of my teachers treated me really well, so my boss should treat me well also.*

Corporate Mindset: *Your teacher treated you well because he was paid to treat you well. Your boss, on the other hand, is paying YOU to make his life easier. Regardless of how he treats you, you earn your paycheck by being useful to him.*

The corporate mindset, summarized, is an anti-entitlement mindset. It is a realization you are responsible for managing your corporate career—no one can do that for you. Someone who has a corporate mindset never lets himself become a victim; martyrs are not appreciated or rewarded at big companies. Optimists—those that refuse to give in to cynicism and bitterness—have a way of coming out on top time and time again.

The corporate mindset also represents a willingness to learn new skills, to observe and adapt. The rules are different in a corporation. In the classroom, there are no layoffs, no bad managers, and no cutthroat cultures. After all, you are paying tuition to be there. It's only logical that the rules change a bit once you start getting paid.

The Power of Reasonable Expectations

When I was relatively junior in my marketing career, I had a senior-level manager say to me, "Sam, in this job you need to make your money before you're fifty, because someday you'll be fired." His comment came as a bit of a shocker to me, to say the least. It did not match the career expectations I had created in my mind while I was in business school. The dissonance it created in me made me feel uneasy. Why in the world would I be fired someday?

Then I started to look around at the people in my department. I noticed two things: First, nearly every employee working there had been with the company for less than ten years, and most of them less than five. Second, there was no one over the age of fifty working there, except the president of the division. My boss was basically right. He wasn't right in the sense that everyone had been "fired." Yet the basic idea behind his comment, that everyone would be gone before they turned fifty, was spot on. The department I worked for had an unwritten "up or out" policy—if you weren't moving up fast enough, then you were out.

What happened to these people after they left? I did some research on that as well, and it wasn't as bad as it sounded. Some people had decided the grind wasn't worth it and decided to leave on their own. Others had been paid illogical sums of money to leave. And yes, others had been kindly told that they need to find another job—and they did.

My manager's comment completely changed my perception of my career at that company. Now, instead of making decisions based on a false perception created in my mind, I finally knew what to expect. You might think that this realization would have been depressing to me. It wasn't. Once I internalized this new reality, I felt liberated. I could now start making plans to succeed in this new, more realistic environment. I could make sure that I kept my career options open and had a lot of contingency plans. I could make sure that I was getting experiences that would make me valuable at other places for when it was time to leave. I could make sure to be smart with my money, building up a reserve of savings in case of emergency. These plans were going to set me up for success.

Of course, not all corporations or departments are this Darwinian. But there are some common patterns of what you can expect when you work for a corporation. Despite different business industries and cultures, corporations share a lot of similarities. Reasonable expectations will help you navigate both the challenges and opportunities that come with corporate life. They will allow you to keep your head up when you feel the sting of temporary disappointment, and to keep your feet on the ground when you experience the exhilaration of temporary success. Understanding how careers typically play out over time is the key to having reasonable expectations.

Here are some things you will likely experience over the life of your successful career:

- Bosses you really connect with who become career-long mentors
- Bosses you don't connect with but learn some useful things from
- Horrible bosses who make you want to quit your job
- Days when you think to yourself, "wow, I can't believe I get paid this much to do this"
- Days when you think to yourself "I really don't get paid enough to deal with all of this"

- Mass layoffs where you keep your job but watch your close friends lose theirs
- Mass layoffs where your friends keep their jobs but watch you lose yours
- Days when you feel extremely valuable and productive
- Days when you think to yourself "I feel like a hamster on a wheel—I work hard and go absolutely nowhere."
- Deep and rewarding friendships with co-workers
- People that you will be happy to never work with again
- Getting promoted into a job you really don't know how to do, but that you figure out
- Not getting promoted when you think you should be
- Getting paid more than you think you are worth
- Getting paid less than you think you are worth
- Coming in at 9 am and leaving at 4 pm because the workload is just that light
- Working insane hours and still feeling behind
- Being put into jobs that you eventually learn are not the right fit for your temperament and skills
- Being put into jobs that are right in the wheelhouse of what you want to do
- Feeling really bad at your job
- Feeling really good at your job
- Traveling to places that you really don't want to go, like Detroit in February
- Traveling to places that you would pay a lot of money to go, like Evian, France, in May
- Managing a high-performing team that makes you look good

- Managing someone who is terrible and a complete drag on your time and productivity
- Strongly disagreeing with key decisions that your company makes
- Working on a growing business
- Working on a declining business
- Working in a toxic culture
- Working in a high-performing culture
- Losing out to a co-worker for a big promotion

I've experienced most of these things over the last ten years, and I expect to experience all of them by the time I retire. None of these things dictates whether an employee succeeds or fails. Successful employees aren't necessarily those who avoid these experiences. Rather, they understand that these experiences are just part of corporate life. This understanding allows them to hold on for the ride and manage through the challenges with a long-term mindset. They recognize that success is determined less by luck and more by their reaction to challenges.

Now that you have a better idea of what to expect from a corporate career, let's move on to building the skills you will need to be successful.

2

SKILL #1: FOCUSING–DISCOVER YOUR POINT OF DIFFERENCE

*Most people have no idea of the giant capacity
we can immediately command when we focus all
of our resources on mastering a single area of
our lives.*

– Tony Robbins

IMAGINE FOR A MOMENT THAT YOU ARE A MID-LEVEL MANAGER at a corporation and your boss is in a conference room with executives from your corporation. The sole purpose of the meeting is to talk about each employee, including you, at your company to determine whose performance is the strongest and who has the most long-term potential. The meeting is one hour long. There are thirty people at your level that they need to discuss in this meeting. Each boss is allotted two minutes to make a pitch for their employee.

After a few minutes, it's your boss's turn—all eyes on him. His job is to make a case for your potential. The outcome of the meeting will determine your near-term pay raise, your bonus, and other perks. More importantly, it will affect your career prospects at your organization for months—even years—to come. After all, the only time the executives talk about you is in this meeting, where your boss gives a two-minute speech.

Does this scare you? It should.

I call this corporate phenomenon "the two-minute rule." It's simple: Your boss must be able to describe why you are valuable in two minutes or less. Because of the fast-paced, time-starved environment in which corporations operate, employees at all levels tend to be known by what is said about them in short, concise conversations. Whether it's in a formal meeting or just simple chatter at the water cooler, people will talk about you. "Is she any good?" They may ask. "Would you want him on your team?" "Is he a good 'fit' here?" "What are her primary strengths and weaknesses?" All these questions are fair game. And when opportunities for new positions—and promotions—come up, those two minutes are of paramount importance.

Now for the critical question: If you are currently working for a corporation, can your boss accurately describe you and why you are valuable in two minutes or less? Or, to take it a level deeper, can you accurately describe to *yourself* why you are valuable to your company? If you answered "no" or "sort of" to the second question, you can just go ahead and say "no" to the first question, too. If you can't succinctly articulate why you are valuable, then your boss certainly won't be able to either.

What's that One Thing?

The key to winning in the "two-minute" environment is focus. How much can be said about you in two minutes? It is enough time for your boss to highlight one—maybe two—key strengths and give a couple of examples for each of them. Those that capitalize on the two-minute rule intuitively understand that, in a competitive, specialized business environment, they must pick and choose what they get good at. They recognize and develop one or two strengths, relentlessly focus on them until they have mastered them, and ultimately become well-known in the organization for them. This creates positive momentum and puts them on an accelerated path to get promoted. Indeed, when focus is applied to the right things at the right time, it can become an incredibly sharp and powerful tool—far more powerful than the blunt tools of raw talent or hard work.

I have spent eight years in the consumer-packaged goods industry, managing everyday brands that you see in the grocery store. A big part of my job is conducting consumer research to better understand the needs and desires of our consumers. For example, I happen to know that when a mom walks down a grocery aisle and stops to consider purchasing a product, she takes an average of three seconds to decide whether or not to put it in the shopping cart. Just three seconds! While that doesn't seem like a lot of time to decide, it's enough for her. What makes her pick one product over another? Clearly, in three seconds, she hasn't had the time to conduct a rigorous analysis of the product's strengths and weaknesses. So she finds one or two things she likes and uses that information to make a decision. Perhaps the color or shape of the package appealed to her. Maybe she is a value shopper and always looks for the lowest price, regardless of brand recognition. Or the photograph of the product on the package could have made it look like the highest-quality option. Maybe some health claims written on the package caught her attention. Regardless of the reason, it is usually just one or two things—not five or six or twenty—that compels a mom to make a purchase.

Great products are great because they are superior to other products in one or two ways. (This is called a "point of difference" in marketing speak.) It might be taste or quality. It could be price. It could be a unique flavor or variety. Decisions are not made from multiple variables. Usually, the product is superior in one or two ways, and that is why it is purchased.

Conversely, products that try to be the best at everything wind up being incredibly mediocre. A product that aims to have the best price *and* the best quality *and* the most variety *and* best customer service just doesn't make sense to consumers. Can you image, for example, if Porsche launched an advertising campaign claiming to be the sports car with the best quality and the best price and the most variety? Such claims would only create disbelief and confusion. The magic in a Porsche is not that it is the best at everything, but that it has deliberately chosen not to be great at some things—low cost, in particular—in order to be excellent at one thing—flawlessly engineered, premium-quality motor vehicles.

Employees are products as well, purchased on the open market with corporate dollars and corporate benefits. A focused employee with a clear selling point commands a much higher premium than an employee who is decent at everything but well-known for nothing.

If you have made it into a large corporation, chances are that you are pretty good at a lot of things. If you are reasonably ambitious, the idea of focusing on developing one or two areas of excellence will make you feel uncomfortable. Nevertheless, in order to obtain true mastery of a skill, you'll have to learn to ignore things. You must stop trying to be good at everything because in doing so you will never be truly great at anything. Greatness is about focus.

This can be a challenge for those who have come from small business or entrepreneurial backgrounds. As an entrepreneur, you are expected to wear a lot of hats. In corporate environments, your job is to do one or two things really well and get other people to do the rest. You have to be able to let go of control and let other people help.

Even for seasoned corporate executives, focusing is extraordinarily difficult. It requires self-discipline and an above-average confidence level. Focused employees do not spend all their time in their comfort zones. For example, they resist the temptation to patrol their emails every five minutes so they can answer non-important messages, just to appear "responsive." Neither do they attend every meeting they are invited to, choosing to opt out of meetings unless it is necessary for them to attend.

Invest Your Time, Don't Manage It

The world has multiple resources that are considered of great value. Water, oil, precious metals, and land fall into this category. But for an employee looking to succeed at a corporation, the most precious resource of all is time. And what a precious resource it is! Unlike other resources, time is fair and equitable. Unlike wealth, good looks, physical strength, and intellectual prowess, which are doled out in seemingly random and unjust ways, time is equally allotted to everyone. Everyone is an equal shareholder with equal voting rights. Shares cannot be sold or exchanged. In this sense, you are on a level playing field with those around you.

Time, like any other resource, can be invested with the intent of gaining a return on that investment. Money managers, for example, seek to invest their money in "high-yield" investments. Just as a money manager evaluates the merits of several investments, so too should you evaluate how to invest your precious time to ensure that you get the highest possible return over the long term. Poor financial managers lose money and get fired, and poor time investors in corporations stagnate and get stuck on the lower rungs of the corporate ladder.

I use the word "invest" deliberately. You should *invest* in time, not *manage* time. The distinction makes a world of difference. Here are some examples of how time investment is different from time management.

Time Management: *There simply aren't enough hours in the day to get everything done that is asked of me. It feels like I get ten new requests added to my list every day and I can never stay on top of it. My schedule is totally packed with meetings and I still have mountains of work to do when I get back to my desk.*

Time Investment: *Not everything that is asked of me is worth doing, so I am selective about which tasks I really put* *effort into. And meetings? I am only the leader or a key contributor in about half of the meetings to which I'm invited. The others are just meetings that I've been pulled into as a courtesy or formality and can easily get out of and have someone send me a quick summary afterward. This frees up more time during my day to do more important things.*

Time Management: *I want to be perceived as someone who is ready and willing to go the extra mile, so I take on extra work when I need to, and I try to give my absolute best to each assignment.*

Time Investment: *While sometimes saying "no" is difficult in the moment, it is extremely liberating afterward. It's amazing that, after I choose to say "no," the organization figures out a way to solve the problem without taking hours of my precious time—hours that I desperately need to spend on other things. With some requests, I won't get away with saying "no," but I recognize that not everything deserves my absolute best. Some tasks just need to be completed with competence. A decent job in half the time will suffice. I'm not being lazy, I'm being smart. I'm still working hard, just on activities that matter more.*

Time Management: *I figure that if I put in more hours and work harder than my competitors, I will eventually come out on top. I have to sacrifice other things in my life right now because I know that at some point I will be at a level where I won't have to work so hard and can spend more time doing the things I love with the people I love.*

Time Investment: *Working more hours than I'm comfortable with for a long period of time sets a negative prece-*

dent within my organization. After a while, they will expect that behavior of me and it will be very difficult to stop working those hours. So I set hours that I am comfortable with and work very hard within that time. If I don't get everything done within that time, then I re-prioritize my tasks. My CEO gets paid fifty times more than I do; there is no way he is working fifty times harder.

Time Management: *I know my weaknesses. I spend a disproportionate amount of timing trying to fix them so that I can be well-rounded.*

Time Investment: *I have a pulse on what I have the potential to be really good at, and what I'm just not wired for. I make sure that I don't have any glaring deficiencies, but I don't try to be great at those things. No matter how much I try, I know others will always be naturally better than me at certain things. I focus on playing to my strengths and leveraging them to get more exposure in my organization.*

Time Management: *I budget every hour in the day to get the maximum amount of efficiency out of my time. Every minute is spoken for. Most of these hours are filled with solving short-term problems or getting answers for people.*

Time Investment: *I keep myself plenty busy, but not too busy. I leave some flexibility in my calendar to capitalize on opportunities that come up to network or take on non-urgent but high-reward projects. I deliberately spend time thinking about problems that my boss would think about and about how I can help solve those problems. I often think about the next three to five years and what I need to do in order to reach my long-term goals.*

Time Management: *I spend a lot of hours studying to make sure I know everything and can speak to the details of my business. I wear a lot of hats and, a lot of times, I know how to do most other people's jobs better than they do.*

Time Investment: *There are few things that I really need to know. The rest can either be looked up or asked of a trusted associate. I know who I need to go to in order to get what I need and they actually like it when I do because I make them feel valued and useful. I value their skills and they value mine. It works out quite nicely.*

The first key to developing the skill of focus is to become a time investor, not a time manager. Time investment is not a matter of talent, charisma, or brains; it is a matter of discipline. You can make daily choices that will free you up to better focus on those things that matter more. Remember that everyone has an equal amount of time, and those that have invested their time wisely will have good things said about them in their two minutes. Those that have only "managed" their time will appear mediocre.

How Do You Know What to Invest In?

Once you have internalized the "time investment" framework, you are ready to choose "high-yield" activities, or the tasks that will generate the best long-term return for you. What exactly are those activities? I regret to tell you that there is no quick answer to help you understand *exactly* what activities you should invest in. There is, however, a framework to help you find the activities best suited to you. High-yield activities at a corporation lie at the intersection of three factors: ability, enjoyment, and relevance.

All three of the factors must be satisfied for it to truly qualify as a high-yield activity. You must have the ability to do it AND you must enjoy doing it AND the organization must value it. Achieving only two of three is not sustainable. Looks what happens if you have only two:

Ability and Enjoyment only: These are the invigorating but non-valuable activities. You have passion and are good at what you do. Unfortunately, the organization doesn't value that activity and will not promote you. To progress at your company, you'll need to re-assess your daily activities and make sure you are working on projects that the organization deeply cares about.

Ability and Relevance only: These are the valuable but miserable activities. You will progress at your company in the short term because you are good at what you do and the organization really values your skills. But you are completely miserable and will eventually burn out or live a life of regret. You are in danger of a very unfulfilling career. Get out fast.

Relevance and Enjoyment only: These activities are enjoyable but below your potential. You will do fine at first but ultimately you may wind up far below your true potential as people with more innate ability will eventually pass you up. Look for other activities that better match your aptitude because that approach will give you the best likelihood of going as far as possible.

Using this framework will help you understand where you should focus. This is not to say that you will only be able to focus on these areas. Every job has a decent amount of drudgery in it; every job has tasks that could be done by someone paid much less than you. The difference is that those who are successful find a way to do fewer of those tasks and focus more on what they know to be their high-yield activities.

The qualifying standards I've laid for a high-yield activity— ability, enjoyment, and relevance—set a high bar. It can be very difficult to find activities that have all three elements. Identifying high-yield activities requires a deep understanding of all areas. Let's take a close look at each.

Ability

As a teenager, I had dreams of becoming a full-fledged rock star. (In fact, I still have that dream.) I knew that I would absolutely love a career like this. Plus, the rock stars that I listened to made plenty of money. My plan was coming together nicely, except for one minor detail: I can't sing. No matter how hard I might try, my voice will never be rock-star quality. Unfortunately, no one with a sound mind would pay to hear me sing on stage.

There is a reason that ability is the first factor to consider when picking your high-yield activities. Taking a hard look in the mirror and assessing your abilities is the first step toward choosing where you should focus. While you gaze into that mirror, you must ask yourself questions like:

- Do I really have better quantitative ability than most of my co-workers?
- Does performing for others come more naturally to me than other people?
- Am I a genuinely creative person?
- Does working with computers come easier to me than most other people?
- Am I better at fixing things around the house than the professional I am paying?

If the answer to these questions is "no," then you should shift your focus on the questions to which you can answer "yes" and invest in those areas. But don't be too harsh on yourself. You do not need to currently be great at something, but you do need to have the natural aptitude to be great.

There is nothing wrong with having hobbies or loving things for which you have mediocre talent. Furthermore, it is good to develop your talent within those areas. I sing rock music in the shower all the time. Heck, I may even be improving a little bit. But I'll never be able to hit the high notes like Steven Tyler or have the wonderful raspy sound of John Lennon. Millions of non-professional basketball players play basketball every day and love it. But most of them will not be able to make it to the NBA and become wealthy. If your goal is to climb the corporate ladder, you must be brutally honest. The world is too competitive not to do what you are naturally good at.

I am not suggesting that we can't become good at things we were once bad at; that grit and determination and hard work don't make a difference. I'm suggesting that capitalizing on your natural talents and abilities will give you the greatest likelihood of success in your corporation and that you should focus your time on these areas.

How do you know if you are good at something? While I will not exhaust all the options for discovering your aptitudes in this book, I will tell you that there are ample resources to help you—aptitude tests, feedback from friends, and trial and error are examples. If you have the desire and combine it with a shred of humility and self-awareness, you will come to understand your strengths and limitations before too long. Sometimes, it's as simple as observing a professional at work and thinking to yourself, "I think I could do that job better."

Relevance

I once worked with an individual who was extraordinarily smart, creative, and personable. We worked together for about a year until I was transferred to another division. A year later, he decided to leave the company. When I spoke with him before leaving, I asked him why he was deciding to leave. He said that his passions lay in things that the company was not interested in. He cared about small, grassroots, off-the-wall innovation. All of his energy and passion went into trying to get ideas for really small ventures off the ground. Unfortunately, this company was a multi-billion-dollar conglomerate, and they weren't too interested in small ventures. In order to pay back their investors, they needed big ideas—multi-million dollar projects that would pay back investors as soon as possible. My friend had the ability and found enjoyment in grassroots innovation ideas that could be turned into new ventures. The company we worked for, however, valued something completely different. He confided in me that in his last performance review before he left the company, his boss had plainly told him, "You have got to stop working on things that nobody cares about."

Your particular skills *must* be valuable to your organization for you to be successful. How can you assess what skills are valued at a company? One way is to understand what functions drive success for the company itself. For example, if you work for Wal-Mart's corporate headquarters, it's a pretty safe bet that you are in the right place if you love the activities related to making things more efficiently through automation—supply chain—or picking out products for other people to purchase—retail buying. Supply chain and merchandising are the lifeblood of that organization. If you work for Dow Chemical, which sells industrial chemical products around the world, you can be sure that selling skills and chemical engineering skills will always be in high demand.

Another approach is to consider the various departments in your organization. Any big company has multiple support functions to support its bread and butter, each requiring a different set of skills. For example, almost every company will have the following departments:

- Sales & Marketing: strong interpersonal skills. A facility with abstract concepts. Ability to adapt to others and navigate ambiguous problems.
- Finance: requires strong analytical skills and linear thinking. High comfort level with numbers.
- Human Resources: keen understanding of human behavior and incentives. Familiarity with legal and other matters.
- Operations: highly process-oriented. Ability to solve problems with multiple variables.

With this approach, you can work for basically any corporation, provided that you are put in the right department.

Enjoyment

This attribute is ignored much more than the other two, but it is perhaps the most important of all three. The prior two factors, ability and relevance, are eventually satisfied by brutal market forces. Not good at building Excel models? You won't succeed in a model-building function. The sales department doesn't care about your accounting skills? You will eventually transfer to a department or company where accounting skill is valued. But enjoyment? Well, you can go through an entire "successful" career and completely ignore the enjoyment factor. No company will stop paying you so long as you are competent at providing what they perceive as a valuable service. In fact, if they value your skills enough, companies might fight to keep you in this position and may even offer more money and a better title just to keep you around. This is extremely dangerous for you because it can lead to a miserable career. As long as you are good at something and your organization values it, you will be kept around and given opportunities in corporations. But you will not be happy.

Some people, in order to stay in jobs they hate, tell themselves myths—also known as lies—to keep themselves going for "just another year or two." But beware: a thirty-five-year career happens one or two years at a time. Before you know it, you'll look back on several miserable years and wonder why you never did anything about it. Do not ignore the enjoyment factor.

Let's look at some of the most common myths people use to ignore the enjoyment factor in their careers:

Myth: The money is too good to pass up. I won't be able to get another job with this kind of salary

Fact: Taking care of yourself and your family is important. You need to make a living. But there is danger in keeping a job based on its salary. Follow the words of Benjamin Franklin (who incidentally had a lot of money): "Money never made a man happy yet, nor will it. The more a man has, the more he wants. Instead of filling a vacuum, it makes one."

Myth: If I sacrifice and keep working long hours at this terrible job for just a little longer, I will eventually get promoted to a better position and it won't be so bad.

Fact: If you hate selling, getting promoted to a better sales job will not bring enjoyment. In fact, often promotions mean additional pressure and stress, which means you will wind up hating it even more.

Myth: Nobody likes their job, that's just the way it is. Work is work, and it's difficult.

Fact: It's true that every job has difficulties, but there is a major difference between having a tough job and a job that you hate. Don't accept the status quo of making a living by doing work you dread.

Myth: *Yes* I hate my job, but I have a great family life and this job supports them.

Fact: Think about how much better your family would be if you came home invigorated and energized from your workday. Rest assured that you will short-change your family emotionally over the long run if you have a miserable career.

Your career won't feel like a thirty-five-year vacation, but it can be fulfilling and enjoyable. You must distinguish between work that you enjoy, even if your actual job has peaks and valleys, and work that you abhor. Even if you are good at it and paid well to do what you hate, it's not worth it.

The Right Context

As you choose to invest in high-yield activities throughout your career, you will be successful and you will get promoted. Yet, as you progress, you must recognize that different activities are required at different levels and then you must be nimble enough to adapt. Along the corporate career ladder continuum, the skills required generally flow from technical to non-technical, concrete to abstract, objective to subjective. In other words, the higher up you get, the more your high-yield activities will involve working with and influencing others. Without developing the skills of working with people, your progression will come to screeching halt. It is good to have technical expertise—especially early in your career but know that at some point your high-yield activities will need to evolve. Conversely, if you see yourself as solely a "people person," you will need to develop some sort of technical or useful skill in the earlier years to succeed. The figure below depicts this career progression continuum.

Your Career

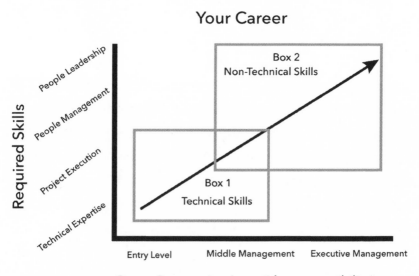

Career Progression (pay, title, responsibility)

Box 1 represents technical expertise. These are the skills taught by universities and trade schools. They are essential skills for a fully-functioning society today, and the world would not operate properly without these skills being applied everywhere every day. More importantly, you need to develop a skill like this in order to get a job. Below are some examples of these skills:

- Computer programing
- Technical writing
- Accounting
- Financial modeling
- Home appraising
- Land Surveying
- Electrical engineering
- Teaching biology
- Data analysis
- Proficiency in business software

People with these skills generally will get jobs and have stable careers. But they will not make it to upper echelons of a corporation without developing the skills found in Box 2. These skills are non-technical and subjective in nature. The Box 2 people are those who have emerged from Box 1 wanting more and willing to pay the price for it. They start to spend less time in the technical details, and more time developing other skills. They are the bosses of those in Box 1. Paradoxically, they may not be as smart as those in Box 1 in terms of raw, processing brainpower, but they are savvy enough to know who wins in business—the Box 2 people. Skills in Box 2 could include the following skills:

- Explaining business issues to co-workers in an understandable way
- Setting a clear and compelling vision

- Bringing out the best in other employees
- Interpersonal relationship skills—connecting with others
- Political maneuvering skills
- Navigating bureaucracy to get things done

This is not to say that you will never need Box 1 again once you reach a certain level. High-yield activities are found in both boxes. But, as you progress, your Box 2 skills become increasingly important. Just keep in mind where you are in your career and, if necessary, adapt. Context is extremely important.

The Decision-Making Framework

I mentioned toward the beginning of this chapter that committing to invest your time in high-yield activities should make you uncomfortable, specifically because you will need the discipline to ignore assignments that waste your time. Corporations are experts at giving you boring and seemingly useless work to do. Some of this work is necessary, like expense reports. It is necessary to complete them to keep your job but virtually useless in helping you toward enhancing your two minutes. In other words, they are necessary to *survive* but they will not help you *thrive*. Again, it's not about eliminating these "survive" activities, but minimizing them so you can focus on thriving. Below is a framework to help you choose high-yield activities on a daily basis.

To illustrate how this works, let's suppose that Jenny has been asked to present her year-end business results to six department directors. Jenny has identified business presentations as one of her high-yield activities. She has the ability to

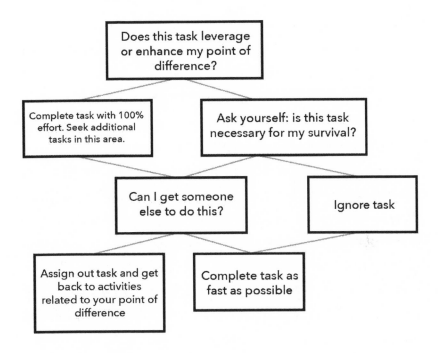

be really good at it, she thoroughly enjoys it, and the company finds it valuable. This is an easy decision for her. She accepts the assignment and will put all her effort into ensuring that her presentation is top-notch.

Now suppose that, two hours later, Jenny has been asked to turn in a production forecast for next quarter. This is not one of her high-yield activities. She is good at it but hates doing it and the organization will never give her extra credit for a job well done. But alas, it is a necessary task for her survival. The first thing she asks herself is whether or not this assignment is necessary for survival or if she can ignore it. She ultimately determines that this satisfactory completion of this task is necessary for her survival—she needs to get done. The next question Jenny asks herself is whether or not she actually has to do it herself. As she thinks about it, she realizes that one of her employees, Rick, is perfectly qualified to do this for her, and so she asks him to do it. Had Rick not been around, Jenny would have hunkered down and completed the job as fast as possible, doing just enough to survive and then getting back to working on her high-yield activity of building her business presentation.

So what is the balance? How much time should be spent on the "survive" activities and how much on the "thrive" activities? There is no clear answer to this question, but what is clear is that many people spend their entire careers only surviving. It's easy to fall into this trap, and you must fight against it. A good benchmark is to strive to spend at least half of your time on your high-yield activities and leave the other half of your time for the other activities. Furthermore, you should dedicate your most productive hours to working on your high-yield activities. Answering emails, for example, does not require your brain to be functioning at maximum capacity. You can still complete that task at the end of the day when your brain is tired.

Imagine the difference in your career if you truly spend half of each working day on the high-yield activities that will help you thrive and make a real difference at your corporation. What would it do for your career over the long term? What impact would it have on your family and other relationships?

Figure out your high-yield activities, and then put systems in place to focus relentlessly on them.

Chapter Summary

- The two-minute rule dictates that successful employees are very good at one or two things and become well-known for them.
- Figure out what you'll be known for and seek to develop those skills.
- To accomplish this, move away from "managing" your time to do everything, and toward "investing" your time in high-yield activities.
- A high-yield activity is an activity that helps you develop your unique skills for which you will stand out at your company.
- High-yield activities have three critical attributes:
  - Ability: Am I good at it?
  - Relevance: Does my organization value it?
  - Enjoyment: Do I like doing it?
- High-yield activities can and should evolve over time; the higher you get, the more the skills involve working with other people.
- Relentlessly discipline yourself by using the decision-making framework to better focus on your high-yield activities.

3

SKILL #2: MANAGING YOUR MANAGER– MASTER THE ART OF FOLLOWERSHIP

If you think your teacher is tough, wait until you get a boss. He doesn't have tenure.
—Falsely attributed to Bill Gates, but worth thinking about nonetheless

"I'M LOOKING FOR A NEW JOB," MY OLD CLASSMATE, BEN, SAID TO me over the phone. It had been two years since we had graduated from business school together and he was calling me to ask about available positions at my company.

"OK Ben, happy to help. Why are you leaving?" I asked. He then told me that he wasn't being fairly compensated for his work relative to his peers.

"So you are leaving because you want more money?" I probed.

"Well, not exactly. I guess I just don't see a lot of upward mobility at my company in the future. I think it will be another year or two before I get promoted and some of my peers are getting promoted this year."

"That's too bad. Why don't you think you'll get promoted if your peers are getting promoted?" I asked, digging deeper.

"Well, if you really want to know, my boss and I don't see eye to eye on a lot of things. She always seems slightly annoyed with me, and I think she is totally unreasonable at times. I don't think she is on my side and, frankly, my life has been pretty miserable since I started working for her a few months ago." He then went on to talk in detail about the challenges he was facing in dealing with his manager.

On and on he went. Once I got him talking about his manager, he didn't stop talking for a very, very long time. It was clear that I had struck a chord with him. The fundamental reason he was looking for a job was that Ben and his boss had a poor relationship. Nothing else seemed to matter.

Ben is not alone. According to a retention study conducted by the Gallup Organization, the number one reason an employee quits a job is the relationship that that employee has with his direct manager.[2] The study goes on to say that at least seventy-five percent of the reasons for leaving jobs can be influenced by managers. As it turns out, the prevailing belief that it's all about the money is wildly inaccurate. Money, as well as benefits, work/life balance, rewards and recognition, opportunities for career advancement, and job security are all very important factors when employees consider job quality. But nothing compares to the daily satisfaction—or misery—that comes from working with your immediate boss.

---

2 *Gallup Business Journal*: "Turning Around Employee Turnover," by Jennifer Robison, May 2008

The relationship you have with your boss is the most important relationship you have at the office. It trumps your relationship with peers, subordinates, people in other departments, and anyone else you work with. If your relationship with your boss is weak, work can be draining, stressful, and downright miserable enough to make you call a headhunter. On the other hand, if it is strong, it can be a fulfilling and invigorating experience. More important, it will put you on a path to winning at your company, ultimately resulting in more promotions and more money in your pocket.

A friend and former co-worker of mine aptly describes the stark difference between a good employee-manager relationship and a bad one. "If you have a bad relationship with your boss, it is like being on a freight train that is climbing a hill," he says. "The train is working tirelessly to gain ground, but any time it lets up just a little bit, it starts sliding backward. The forces of gravity pull it back and it loses momentum. On the other hand, a good employee-manager relationship is like being on a train going downhill. The train has plenty of momentum and can even ease off the gas a little and still coast forward."

The power of momentum in large companies cannot be underestimated. When you have negative momentum, you get way more blame than you deserve. When you have positive momentum, you get way more credit than you deserve. Having a great manager-employee relationship is a critical component of building positive momentum in your career.

Who is Getting Paid?

Before diving into the critical behaviors that will ensure that you have a successful relationship with your manager, we must return to the principle of the corporate mindset. Recall that in Chapter 1 we discussed the difference between the school mindset and real-world mindset. The school mindset assumes the world is like a big classroom, where everything is laid out in a syllabus and every answer to a problem can be found in a textbook. The real-world mindset is the opposite. It recognizes that answers aren't always clean-cut and that most problems aren't solved by reading a manual. In the real world, you are expected to figure things out on your own.

Which mindset is more appealing? To me, I would take the school mindset any day of the week. (In fact, some days I wish I could go back to school!) Life according to the school mindset is easier, and for one simple reason: In school, you are *paying* (either through tuition or your parent's taxes), while in the real world, you are *getting paid*.

Several years ago, I was boarding an airplane on my way home from a business trip. The flight had been delayed a few hours due to airline errors. As we stepped onto the plane, a man standing in front of me expressed his frustration about the delays to the flight attendant. The flight attendant listened to the man and then promptly responded in an irritated voice, "You know, I'm just as upset with this airline as you are, so don't complain to me." Shocked at the flight attendant's response, the man quickly replied, "Yeah, but I'm paying, and you're getting paid! Don't complain to *ME*, lady!"

In business—and in life—it is always helpful to consider who is writing the checks and who is cashing them. Certain behavior is expected of people who are getting paid. In my example, the flight attendant's words may have been true. They may have given her extra shifts or perhaps the pilots had been extra bossy that day. She may have had every right to be upset with the airline. Yet regardless of how her day was going, she was the one getting paid and thus was expected to help those that were paying.

Now, consider your relationship with your manager. If you were to approach things as if you were in school, you would assume that your manager is like a professor, someone paid to teach you and help you succeed. If they aren't doing their job, you can tell your parents or report them to the dean's office, and they actually have to listen. The real world is the reverse. You will succeed not by complaining about your manager, but by helping your manager succeed. If you don't like your manager, that's your problem. Rarely will anyone at the company be interested in listening to why your manager stinks. In fact, if you go to your manager's boss to express your disapproval, this tactic will likely backfire on you, sparking an even worse relationship with your manager. Having the school mindset with your boss will weaken your momentum.

There is one exception to this. If your manager is engaged in any sort of unethical, illegal, or immoral activity, you should report that behavior to human resources. Examples of this could include racist or sexist comments, bullying, misuse of corporate funds, or major conflicts of interest actions that clearly breach contracts. Your company should have a corporate hotline that you can call anonymously for these types of problems.

In the real world, however, you are getting paid, and therefore you are responsible to make sure that your relationship with your boss is strong. It is not your manager's responsibility to make sure it is strong; it is not the HR department's responsibility; it is not your corporation's responsibility; it is YOUR responsibility. Do not leave the most important relationship in your career in someone else's hands. Take control of your own destiny by managing your manager.

The Success Equation

If you ask ten people to define success, you will likely get ten different answers. But when it comes to succeeding with your manager, there is only one definition. It can be succinctly articulated by the following equation:

$$\text{Success} = \frac{\text{Performance}}{\text{Expectations}}$$

Your goal should be to have the highest success score possible with your boss. There are two ways to gain a high score. The first is to increase performance; the second is to reduce expectations. Most employees put way too much focus on the numerator of this equation, working harder and harder, failing to push back on anything requested of them. Too few employees focus enough on managing expectations appropriately. This gets them into trouble. Here are the keys to managing expectations with your boss:

Be careful what you sign up for: It is a good employee's inclination to be optimistic about future outcomes to avoid unpleasant conversations. But it's much better to under-sell and over-deliver. Make sure you are confident that you can deliver what you commit to.

Fight for reasonable timelines: Many times, bosses ask for things before they actually need them. If you have good logic for asking for more time, do it. It's better to give yourself enough time to commit to a job well done than say yes to an unreasonable timeline and deliver sub-par work.

Constantly communicate priorities: When things get tight and you feel overwhelmed, make sure to tell your boss exactly what is on your plate and what things you are putting first. Many times, your boss will tell you to stop working on something that you previously thought was important. Other times, he will switch your priorities around. In either case, you will make sure he is comfortable with how you are approaching your work.

Make Your Boss Look Good

What does your manager most desire? Strong business results? More money? More recognition? Leadership opportunities? Corporate perks? The gratification of mentoring and teaching others? He probably wants all of the above. But there is one thing your manager wants more than anything else; one thing that he believes leads to all the other things. And that one thing is this: Your manager wants to look good in front of his manager. He wants to look smart, competent, and strategic. He wants to look like he is masterfully managing his responsibilities and that he can be depended on to deliver results. He wants to look like he understands the challenges and opportunities that face him and that he has contingency plans for any risks in his business. He wants his boss to trust him. He feels that, if he is in a good place with his boss, then he has a bright future at his company.

Your objective, then, is to make sure that your boss looks good in front of others—especially his boss. Below is how you can accomplish this.

No surprises: "I hate surprises," is one of the most familiar phrases echoed in corporate halls. No manager likes surprises—especially if his boss finds out before he does. Why? Because surprises, in general, tend to make people look stupid and unprepared in front of their bosses. Managers hate looking stupid in front of their bosses! So, you need to keep your manager informed constantly. How do you know what to tell your boss and what not to tell your boss? Use this benchmark: If your manager's manager would care about this if they found out, then you should tell your boss. When in doubt, communicate! It's better to let your boss tell you that you can stop communicating so much than to fail to tell him about some biggies.

Sometimes people want to not tell their boss something because they think they'll be able to solve the problem without the boss ever finding out. If you have a high level of confidence that you'll solve the problem quickly, then go ahead. But there is nothing wrong with communicating an issue with your boss and telling them how you are going to solve it. This, at a minimum, covers you in case something blows up.

Deliver bad news quickly: You will not be able to avoid bad news—but do not sweep it under the carpet and hope it will go away. Bad news has a funny way of re-appearing if not promptly addressed. Not telling your boss about it quickly is like letting an infected wound fester and spread until it becomes life-threatening. Telling your boss immediately is like applying alcohol to the wound: It stings a little bit at first, but begins the healing process immediately, and prevents further damage.

You do not need to wait for a formal meeting to break bad news to your boss. It can simply be "Hey, I know you're busy, but I just need to talk to you about something so you are not caught off guard." This will help your boss know that you are looking out for her and want her to maintain her credibility with her boss and peers.

Deliver bad news correctly: Bad news is, well, bad. Your boss doesn't want to hear it and you don't want to give it. Given this sensitivity, here are some guidelines to help you deliver it. Make sure you have poise, the right amount of detail, and a recommended solution.

Poise: When something bad has happened at work, it may completely stress you out. A customer worth 20% of your business has discontinued your product line; a large client has asked you to deliver your recommendations a month earlier than expected; you have to recall a new toy because it has been proven to be unsafe for children. Whatever the problem and no matter how stressful, you cannot walk into your boss's office unglued. Show concern, but have the maturity to keep your composure. If you need to take a few minutes to compose yourself and think through your talking points, it's worth it to take them.

Detail: Give enough information to show that you have properly diagnosed the problem. What is the background? What are the relevant facts? Have you talked with the key people involved? What do they say? What impact will it have on the business and what does it mean? You do not need to give a great amount of detail. Just give the most relevant facts that he needs to know to pass on to his boss. If he wants more detail, let him ask for it. If he asks you a question that you don't know the answer to, just say "I don't know that yet, but I'll communicate that once I know. I am still in the process of digging into everything but I felt like it was most important to at least give you a heads up about this now."

Solution: Until this point, you have an imaginary sign on your forehead that reads "I am part of the problem." After all, you are the person who walked in on your boss's perfectly good day and dropped a bomb. To get this sign off your head, you need to walk into your boss with a recommendation on how to solve this problem. You do not have to have a fully fleshed-out solution. Just bring some options and your recommendation. This engages your boss and lets her know that you are part of the solution, not part of the problem.

Here is a real-life example of how to communicate with poise, detail, and with a solution:

Jenn works as a regional sales manager for a multinational medical device company. She handles all the accounts in two large retail cities. One morning, Jenn gets a phone call. It's the buyer from her biggest customer. She tells them that they have decided to stop carrying her biggest-selling pacemaker product because a competitor has offered a lower price. After the call, Jenn tries to sort through in her mind the best way to break the news to her boss.

RESPONSE #1:

Directly after hanging up the phone with the buyer, Jenn frantically walks into Tom's office looking flustered. "Tom, guess what? Our biggest customer just discontinued the pacemaker. I just can't believe it! How could they do this? They said it's because they got a better deal somewhere else. I guess they went with our biggest competitor. Seriously, they've been undercutting us all year and I'm sick of it. After all these years with us, they've decided to sell out. I've had it with them, and I've had it with this job!"

How would you grade Jenn on her poise, level of detail, and recommended solutions?

Poise: Because Jenn is so flustered, Tom is thinking that Jenn can't hack it when things go wrong. He makes a mental note in his mind to tell her in her next performance review to maintain more composure and show more business maturity under pressure.

Detail: The only thing Tom knows at this point is that a big product has been discontinued and that his sales manager has come unglued.

Solutions: Unless complaining about her customer counts as a recommendation, Jenn has nothing.

RESPONSE #2:

After hanging up the phone, Jenn's initial reaction is frustration and disbelief. But she takes a deep breath and thinks it over for a couple of hours. She takes some time to jot down her talking points. Feeling more prepared, she approaches Tom:

"Tom, I just found out some tough news, do you have ten minutes to talk about it?" she says. "Sure, but only have five minutes," Tom replies. "Great. I will keep it to five minutes for you now and will set up more time on your calendar to go through the detail. I just wanted to make sure you knew about this right away. OK, so here's what happened. A couple of hours ago I got a call from my biggest customer saying that they are planning to discontinue our pacemakers effective next month. The reason she gave was that another supplier had offered a better price and they took it. Something tells me that this isn't the entire story so I am investigating further and expect to have an answer to you by end of week. If this were to happen:

1. We would lose $3 million in sales or about 15% of my total business.
2. The manufacturing plant would likely lay off 10% of employees.
3. There could be a ripple effect of losing other customers.

Clearly, I'm disappointed. This presents a real challenge to our business. But I don't think we're out of the game yet, Tom. I've put together an action plan to make sure we don't lose this business. Here it is:

1. Conduct a competitive assessment to assess what price our competitor has likely given.
2. Analyze what our business impact would be if we matched their price.

3. *Brainstorm other ways we could entice them to keep our pacemakers outside of price, including product improvements or additional service perks.*

These are my initial thoughts. Since this issue needs to be resolved quickly, I expect to be back in front of you by early next week to show you our game plan. For now, I'd like to hear any initial reactions or suggestions that you may have based on what I've just told you.

How about now?

Poise: She showed concern and accountability, but kept her composure and stuck to the facts. Even if she felt personal betrayal from the buyer, she didn't show it too much. (There is nothing wrong with showing a little emotion and passion, but showing too much can make you counter-productive.)

Detail: She gave the details that Tom cared about, but not too many details. Remember, too much detail can just raise more questions. Relevant details are usually the ones that help your boss understand what happened, why, and what it means for the business. Now is not the time to show off how many facts you know about your business.

Solution: Jenn had developed some options for potential solutions. She didn't ram a solution down Tom's throat. This is the first time Tom has heard this, so he needs time to digest. The key here is to show him that you are already working on solutions and have some potential options. The final recommendation can be given the next week.

If you can't remember the three keys to giving your boss bad news (poise, details, and solution), here is a more practical way: Simply ask yourself, does my boss now feel comfortable going into her boss to deliver the bad news? In the first example, not only did Tom not know the important facts, but he had no solutions to recommend and no confidence that Jen was able to fix it. In the second example, Tom had a pristine story. Tom will look good in front of his boss and not have to do any additional work. Get ready for that promotion!

Find ways to deliver good news: Your goal is to minimize negative experiences and maximize positive experiences with your boss. Don't just stop in when something bad happens. Find ways to celebrate little wins. Send emails often of positive experiences, even if they are small.

Stay positive: Never, ever say anything bad about your boss or your current job. Talking negatively about your boss will eventually come back to bite you. If you tell business associates, suppliers, or local friends that you don't like your manager, you run the risk of your boss finding out. And when she does, she will feel threatened. Never forget that at large companies, a big part of a manager's job is to help those under them to be successful. In fact, it's part of how they are individually evaluated. When your boss hears that someone under him is unhappy, he will feel like he is underperforming and get worried that his boss will find out. That is why it's just better to keep negative feelings about your job to yourself. The only exception to this rule would be your spouse or out-of-town relatives. After all, you need to vent to someone.

Maximize "mind time:" Forget everything you've heard about the "new economy" and that face time doesn't matter anymore. Rubbish! You should always seek to get face time with your boss. Yet with all the technological change of the last thirty years, face time should be renamed "mind time." Communication with your boss can happen via email, text messaging, video conferencing, or actual face-to-face interactions. However you choose to do it (more importantly, how your boss prefers it), you should maximize interaction with your manager for three reasons. First, you'll be on his mind when things come up, and you will naturally get more involved in solving business problems and taking on more responsibility. Second, you will learn from and be mentored by him. Third, you will show your commitment to work. Even though you may not be working any more hours than anyone else, it will sure seem like it to your boss.

Tell your boss you enjoy working for him: If all else fails, just try good old-fashioned flattery! Who doesn't like to be liked? Who doesn't like to be told they are good at what they do? Your boss is a mortal, and just as subject to vanity as anyone else. I'm not suggesting you lie if your boss is terrible, but it is rare that you hate everything about them. Find something good about your boss and highlight it.

Managing Salary and Promotion Conversations

When it comes to pay and promotion, your boss will be either your biggest advocate or your biggest deterrent. The primary metric that the organization will use when deciding to promote you will be whether or not your boss thinks you deserve it. When you are really junior in your career, your boss simply may have the power to pull the trigger for your promotion—or stop it dead in its tracks—at any time. As you grow into more senior positions, other people, like your peers, your boss's peers, and people in other departments may be able to weigh in. Still, at any level, the organization will rely heavily on your boss's opinion. If your boss thinks you are ready, you will generally get the nod.

The fatal flaw so many employees make is to not actively talk about pay and promotion with their bosses. They wrongly assume that if they are doing what they are asked, they will get promoted. One reason for this is that they are still stuck in the school mindset, assuming that promotions are like moving from sophomore to junior year in high school—as long as they don't flunk out of any classes, they will automatically be moved onto the next level. This assumption is grossly false. Corporations are obligated to be smart with their finances, and salary payments are a big expense.

The second reason employees don't bring it up is plain and simple fear. They don't want to cause friction or damage the relationship. Or, they are afraid that the answer will be "You do not get a pay raise or a promotion this year." They don't like the idea of hearing this, so they spare themselves the discomfort and don't ask, figuring that if their boss wants to promote them, then it will be a pleasant surprise.

You must actively discuss promotion with your boss. Employees who are promoted actively talk with their bosses about their development and push the issue. As the saying goes, "The squeaky wheel gets the grease." Here are some guidelines for having these conversations:

Twice a year: You should have formal pay and promotion discussions approximately twice a year. The best time to bring it up is generally in a performance review. You can certainly have less formal discussions more often than that when you think it is necessary. Every time you have a promotion discussion, you should start where you left off, highlighting what was talked about and agreed to in the previous discussion.

Have plenty of ammunition: If you think you deserve a promotion or pay raise, you must bring sound logic and facts to back it up. This could include market research showing that you are worth more in the marketplace or evidence that you are performing at the next level according to job descriptions at that level. Also, while virtually all corporations claim they are meritocracies, seniority still plays a big role. If you have been in a job for a long time, that should work in your favor.

You can also use the power of comparison. While comparing yourself to others is not a great life strategy to achieve happiness, it works very well when talking about promotions. Understanding your tenure and performance against your peers will help you make your case. Corporations care about this because they care about managing fairness across their organization. They also don't want good people to feel like they've been mistreated and resign. Don't disparage your peers, but talk factually. If you have been there two years longer than someone who was promoted before you, it's fair to kindly ask for an explanation.

Do not, however, tell them you should be promoted because you need the money or because of inflation or anything that puts you in a position to show personal weakness. Always focus on facts that support why you deserve it.

And lastly, always ask for a little more than you are comfortable with. Corporations rarely give you everything you ask for. After all, it's a negotiation, with some give and take, so anchor high.

Managing Disagreements with Your Manager

There are certain times that you will simply not agree with your boss on certain issues. In this case, you should be careful to not take a hardline stance of opposition with him in highly visible public meetings or in front of others. You need to always support him in these instances and never challenge his credibility or make him feel threatened. However, if you have a real concern with his decisions or what he is asking you to do, you should not let it fester and should talk to him about it.

The best way to do this is to set up a separate meeting to address the issue. Bring data to talk about why you disagree with a decision and a recommendation as to what you think would be a better course of action. Finally, always reaffirm that you fully support him and whatever he decides, but that you felt obligated to share your opinions with him.

If, after you have done this and your boss has not changed his mind, there is only one thing for you to do: do what he says. After all, they don't call him "boss" for nothing. You are being paid to do what he says, so do it. And do it with your full support. You have had the discussion with him and said what you wanted to say. Dragging your feet after that would only hurt your career.

Handling Irreconcilable Differences

What if you have tried and tried and you know deep inside that you and your boss will never be able to get along? This is a tough situation for you because you will almost never win against your boss. Unless there is unethical or improper behavior, count on the organization taking your boss's side. He is higher in the corporate pecking order and therefore has more rights and privileges than you do. Don't try to launch a battle to oust your boss or take away his credibility. It will only reflect poorly on you.

When you are stuck in this predicament, you have three choices:

1. **Leave the company:** Switching jobs in your career is not necessarily a bad thing, but leaving solely because you can't stand your boss is a poor reason. First, you have no guarantee that you'll like your new company and boss any better. Second, staying at your company may be the best option for you long term, but you just can't see it because your relationship with your boss gives you a pit in your stomach every morning when you wake up. Step back, take a deep breath and realize that other factors, like longevity at your company, a job that aligns with your skills, and the best location fit for your family are way more important factors to consider than your current boss. We'll deal with reasons to switch jobs later on. The material point is, don't do anything rash just because your current day-to-day work is temporarily unenjoyable.

2. **Request a transfer:** This is a viable strategy if you like your company, and if you have time to investigate potential bosses before attempting to make a switch. You can either apply to internal job postings or come up with your own idea for a job and pitch it. In this case, I recommend setting up a meeting with a mentor—some-

one with more experience and clout than you—that you trust in the company and ask for help in getting it done. It may require setting up confidential meetings with your potential new boss and persuading him or her to hire you. But be extra careful. When making your pitch, put together a logical business case for why it is good for your development and what you will bring to the table. Never simply say that you are trying to get away from your boss. Your new potential boss is not in the business of doing you favors, so speak mostly in terms of their needs.

3. **Wait it out:** You will likely not have to deal with your boss for more than two years. According to a 2012 longitudinal study conducted by the Bureau of Labor Statistics, the average person born in the latter years of the baby boom (1957-1964) held 11.3 jobs from age eighteen to forty-six[3]. That's once every 2.5 years! And that doesn't include switching positions at the same company. For comparison, I've been in at my most recent company for three years and have had three bosses. So hang in there. You can do anything for a year or two.

Throughout your career, you are likely to have multiple bosses. Learn everything you can from them, good and bad. If anything, you can make promises to yourself about things you'll never do when you are the boss.

---

3 See BLS News Release "Re/ sults from Longitudinal Study" Wednesday, July 25, 2012

Chapter Summary

- Your relationship with your boss is the most important relationship you have at work.
- Your boss is not your professor. You paid your professors to be good to you. Your boss pays you to be good to him.
- The success equation is **Success = performance/expectations.** Focus just as much on managing expectations as you do on managing your performance. You can manage expectations by :
  - Being careful with what you sign up for
  - Fighting for reasonable timelines
  - Constantly communicating priorities
- Make your boss look good by:
  - Minimizing surprises
  - Delivering bad news quickly
  - Delivering bad news with poise, details, and solutions
  - Finding ways to deliver good news
  - Staying positive
  - Maximizing mind time
  - Telling your boss you like working for him
- Proactively manage your career by:
  - Having promotion conversations with your boss at least twice per year
    - Having plenty of market-based ammunition, including market data and comparison with your peers
    - Staying away from talking about your needs, but focusing on the marketplace

- When you disagree with your boss on something serious, have a private conversation with your boss to resolve the issue; don't let it fester and don't bring it up in the wrong place
- If you have irreconcilable differences with your boss, you have the following options:
  - Leave the company
  - Request a transfer
  - Wait it out

4

SKILL #3: BUSINESS STORYTELLING–MAKE DATA INTERESTING AND PERSUASIVE

D URING MY FIRST YEAR OF WORKING AS AN ASSOCIATE BRAND manager for ConAgra Foods, a $12 billion food conglomerate, I was asked to join a "high-profile" project sponsored by the president of the Frozen Foods Division. I was out of town visiting a customer when my vice-president called to tell me about it.

"Get on the next available flight home today," he said.

"But I'm not supposed to fly out until tomorrow, boss," I responded.

"It doesn't matter. I'm relieving you of your current assignments and pulling you into a project. This project is now your number one priority. Get home tonight and be in my office tomorrow at 8 am."

The next morning I was back at corporate headquarters, sitting in my VP's office, signing confidentiality documents. Then my boss explained the details of the project. ConAgra was considering buying another business and needed someone to analyze the pros and cons of doing the deal. Senior leadership cared a lot about this project and I was going to get an opportunity to present my recommendation to them. This was my opportunity to make an impression and enhance my "two minutes." If, however, I were to completely bomb my presentation, it could be a big stain on my career at that company. My VP confirmed this when he gave me his final piece of advice on the project: "Don't screw it up."

I dug into the project. It was big and complex, with tens of millions of dollars on the line. I had a week to pull together my analysis for my boss and then another couple of days to refine it for the division president. There would be a significant amount of number crunching and analysis involved. Although intimidated, I was determined to succeed. I set out that week pouring through countless data files and carefully analyzing them. I worked with experts in different departments to understand the parts of the business that applied to this potential acquisition. The amount of detail was overwhelming, but I diligently captured all of the relevant data points for my final report.

After a long, arduous week, I sat again with my VP to show him everything that I had done. I took him through the numbers and how I arrived at them, detailing each nuance in the data and explaining why they were correct. He sat patiently and listened to me until I was finished. He then congratulated me on my diligent analysis and applauded my analytical work. He even called me an Excel nerd—which I think he meant as a compliment. Then he paused, grinned, and taught me a valuable business lesson:

"Sam, at some point, it's not so much about what you are saying, but how you say it," he said. He then told me that my work lacked a vital element: a clear story. I had plenty of data, but it wasn't telling him to do anything. He nicely told me that I was not ready to show my work to the president, because all the president would have to say at the end of my presentation was "So what? Do you think I should buy this business? Why?" Getting up in front of my president with a lot of data and little to say about it would make for a mediocre presentation.

Fortunately, my boss was a great mentor. "I'm not going to let you fail," he said. He spent thirty minutes helping me craft the right story and then sent me on my way. I had a couple of days left, which I used to practice like crazy. The day of the presentation came and I was anxious. When I got to the conference room, the executive team was standing in a buffet line to grab some lunch that had been brought in for the meeting. I jumped in line right next to the division president. This man was notorious for his poker face and lack of small talk. Chit-chat was not his thing. We stood in awkward silence for a moment, when my VP approached us and said with his usual grin, "Just so you know, Sam is *really* nervous."

Thanks for the ice-breaker.

After what seemed like a three-hour lunch, I stood and delivered my presentation. Throughout the presentation, I was amazed at how few questions I got from the president about the data. He quickly digested the data and main facts but almost the entire discussion centered on my point of view—my story. "Did I really think we are the right company for this product line? Why did I think we could grow the business? How would our sales force react to this acquisition? Besides the numbers, what other things should be considered?" I had been prepped by my boss to answer most of these questions, so fortunately I always had a response.

After I was done answering questions, I sat down. I couldn't tell whether or not I had done a good job or completely tanked.

My president was still poker-faced, and my VP sat with his usual grin. Finally, when the meeting adjourned, I got the reward I was looking for. The president stood up, and on his way out looked at me and said, "This is really good. Good job." I knew this man well enough to know that free compliments weren't his thing. I left the conference room feeling great.

My VP and mentor saved me that day by teaching me the value of a clear story. Without a story, my presentation would have fallen flat. But with my story in hand, I had something to say. I learned that it wasn't about having all the data memorized, but having a well-reasoned opinion. Whether my president agreed with me or not, I had a story to tell, and that is what mattered.

Storytelling Versus Data-Telling

The proliferation of technology over the last half-century has created a data surplus in business today. Corporate servers store terabytes of data that can be accessed at any time and place. Spreadsheets that once took up precious real estate in filing cabinets now hardly make a dent in electronic storage. Armies of analysts are employed with the sole task of slicing and dicing data using complex software. "Big Data" has emerged as one of the most prominent business buzzwords of the last 10 years.

A surplus, by definition, is having more of a resource than is required. The problem with surpluses is that they present the temptation to over-consume. In food surpluses, for example, overconsumption creates a series of health problems like obesity, diabetes, and heart failure. In business, the symptoms of over-consuming data are a little different, but still damaging nonetheless. Overconsumption of data at corporations can cause confusion, frustration, wasted time and money, and decreased morale. In corporations, the words used to express these symptoms are "spinning," "churn," and "analysis paralysis." *Consuming* data for its own sake is not a healthy practice in business today.

Even while corporations operate with a data surplus, they suffer from a critical deficiency at the same time. The shortfall that plagues corporations today is that of clear stories—stories that take facts and data and turn them into action. A shortfall is the opposite of a surplus and is defined as having fewer resources than required. Just like surpluses, shortfalls contain their fair share of negative symptoms. Back to my food example, food shortages can cause malnourishment, diseases, crime, riots, war, and a host of other societal challenges. In business, a shortfall of clear business stories causes stagnation, mass confusion, and, ultimately, losing in the marketplace. Without clear business stories, businesses do not have a way to move forward.

With the surplus of data in business comes a glut of "data-tellers," those who slice and dice data, and then regurgitate and spread it across their organizations like a virus. These employees are abundant. Large corporations don't need more of them, even if they think they do. What organizations desperately need, however, are storytellers—those who can take the relevant data and make something of it. Good storytellers are scarce in organizations, but data tellers are in high supply. Basic economics will tell you that scarce resources command higher prices than surplus resources. So too, will you, if you can tell excellent stories.

I'm not discounting the importance of facts and data in organizations. Big organizations are inherently conservative and thus need data and facts to feel comfortable about their decisions. But business is not like bookkeeping, mathematics, or technical writing. In those fields, there is generally a "correct" answer. But not in business. In large companies, the one who has the best story wins. Stories often include data, but the data play a *supporting* role, not a dominant one. To make a home-building analogy, the story is the foundation and framing, and the facts and data are all the finishings, like drywall, paint, and light fixtures. With a good foundation and a solid frame, you still have a house that stands. But all the drywall and paint in the world won't do you any good without the fundamentals of a foundation and frame. Similarly, a good story can do a reasonable job of hiding weak data. But no amount of data can make up for a bad story.

Storytelling requires a different mindset than data-telling. Consider the following examples of the data-telling mindset, and how it differs from the storytelling mindset.

Data-Telling: When trying to prove a point to a co-worker, I use as many facts as possible so that my argument is irrefutable.

Story Telling: I only want the relevant data that support my main point. Throwing superfluous data at someone only confuses them.

Data-Telling: When I approach my boss about a tough business decision that needs to be made, it is my job to gather as much data as possible and give it to my boss to help her make a decision.

Story Telling: It is my job to provide solutions for my boss, so when a tough business decision must be made, I will go into my boss with a recommendation on what we should do. I may use data to back up my decision, but only if it directly supports my point of view.

Data-Telling: When making a big presentation to a lot of people, I make sure to use a lot of charts to show them that I'm smart and thorough.

Story Telling: I first consider my audience and what I'm trying to accomplish and then I create a story that works. I will use simple data to really drive home my key points but the data must be easy to digest to everyone in the audience. My rule is that the dumbest person in the room needs to be able to interpret it within a few seconds of seeing it.

Data-Telling: When executives pass me in the hall and ask me how my business is doing, I recite to them my latest quarterly results or sales figures. This shows them that I know what is going on in my business.

Story Telling: Executives generally know my results and, if they don't, they have no context when you rattle them off. I include my results, but make sure I add to my story like what is going really well and why, what my biggest challenges are, and what I'm doing to fix them.

Principles of Telling Stories with Data

Most business stories at large corporations require some sort of data to go along with them. This is not because data makes stories more exciting and entertaining but because it makes them more credible. Again, big companies need the security blanket of data to help them along in their decisions. But just because your story includes data doesn't mean that it can't be interesting, engaging, and compelling. Here are some key elements of building a great business story with data. These principles can be used whether you are making a formal presentation, passing your boss in the hallway, or conducting a meeting over the phone with another department.

#1: It's okay to be biased: Here is a multiple choice question for you: What is the purpose of storytelling at work?

    a. Educate

    b. Persuade

    c. Entertain.

The correct answer is B—to persuade. Corporations exist because they sell something that other people want to buy. Make no mistake, corporations have an agenda that they are pushing and that is totally okay.

#2: Story first, data second: Before analyzing a single data point, sit down and create the skeleton of your story. Use your brain and gut to develop some hypotheses and then ask yourself the facts you need to find in order to prove or disprove them. Never jump into the data with the hope that it will create a story for you—that's your job. Create the story first and then find the facts to support it. If you create a story and the facts don't support it, then go back and create another story. Starting with your story first will save you hours of time.

John Lasseter, co-founder of Pixar, said, "No amount of great animation can save a bad story." This saying holds true when you replace the word "animation," with the word "data." Ideally, you have solid data and a great story but if you have to make trade-offs, you want your story to be buttoned up first. If you go to your boss with a great story and weak data, you'll likely be okay; if you go in with great data but no story, get ready for mass confusion.

#3: Adapt to your audience: Abysmal presentations are rarely abysmal because of poor content; the content is almost always strong. The failure comes from not understanding what the audience cares about.

Suppose you are required to give three separate business updates to the following individuals: Your direct manager, the president of your division, and a friend in another department. Each presentation is scheduled at a different time. Do you think you can give the same presentation to all three people? If you did, you would surely confuse one person and bore another.

As you prepare your presentation in the context of your audience, it helps to think about the following factors that will affect how you present:

	Direct Manager	President of Division	Friend in Another Department
Time	Medium	Low	Medium
Level of Detail	Medium	Low	Medium
Formality	Low	High	Low
Context Required	Low	Medium	High

It's not an exact science, but this can help you structure a presentation that doesn't either confuse or bore people.

#4: Make data relatable: Data and facts are cold and dry. Warm them up by making them real for people. For example, rather than tell people that 33% of American children are malnourished, tell them to think of the kids in their neighborhood. Then tell them that one in three of those kids they know is likely feeling really hungry right now. Or, rather than talk about how unemployment is at an all-time high, talk about your brother-in-law who has been out of a job for six months.

#5: Keep it simple: Have as many backup charts as you want but, when you are telling your story, keep the data very simple. People generally don't want to dig deep into the numbers; they just want to know that you've done your research.

Give them a few compelling facts that they can write home about and then call it good.

Exercise: Below are two business scenarios, each with a data-telling response and storytelling response. Imagine that you are the audience for the story. Imagine that you are in the audience. Which one would you rather hear?

The Storytelling Framework

Our natural tendency as human beings is to tell stories the same way I explain to my wife why I've just spent $300 on camping equipment. It goes something like this:

"Honey, you'll never believe the great deal I just got. Okay, so you remember how I've been looking for a new tent for a long time? Well, I finally decided to start really looking hard. I have been to three or four stores in the past couple of weeks and just couldn't find something for the right price. Well, yesterday I got an email from REI, saying that there would be a sale today. Now, I know REI is pretty expensive, but it's really good quality stuff that will last for a long time. I mean, anything I buy there could be used for family camping trips. Plus, each of our kids can use this stuff for their future scouting trips. Anyway, I looked at four or five different options but ultimately decided this one four-man tent would be best for our family camping trips. So I bought it. The good news is that REI has a great return policy so after I set it up, if you or the kids don't like it, I can just take it back."

"And guess what, it normally costs $400, but guess how much I got it for? Guess? That's right, $300!

Of course, Gina wanted to hear very little of that story. The only thing she cared about was 1) what I bought, and 2) how much did it cost? She couldn't care less about the back story.

At work, we like to tell stories the same way, preparing the listener for the good or bad news we're going to give them, setting things up with way too much back story, without even a thought of prioritizing our message.

Your co-workers, including your boss and corporate executives, want to hear stories exactly opposite from the way we like to tell them. They want to hear a story the way I would talk to my wife after I've been in a car accident with the kids and call her to let you know.

"Honey, we've been in a car accident, but the kids and I are fine. Now, let me explain what happened...."

Can you imagine if this had happened and I had left "the kids and I are fine" to the very end of the story? Gina would have screamed into the phone within five seconds "Are the kids OK!" No other facts would matter until I gave her that information.

To some extent, that is how your co-workers feel when you are giving them information with too much detail and back story without giving them your key message.

How we like to tell stories—the camping equipment model:

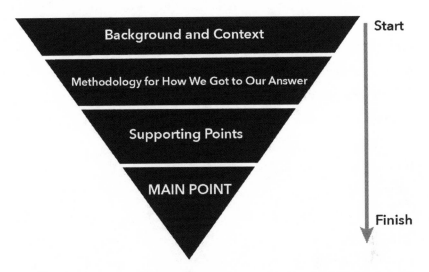

How your co-workers want to hear stories—the car accident model:

If you are a filmmaker or author, you may find it more effective to tell stories differently and even leave your key main point to the end. Entertainment plays by a different set of rules. But, as a businessperson, you should almost always use the "car accident" storytelling model.

I teach a course on storytelling to junior-level marketing employees at my company. In the course, I give them a storytelling framework to help them think through how to structure telling their story successfully.

Each part of the framework works as follows:

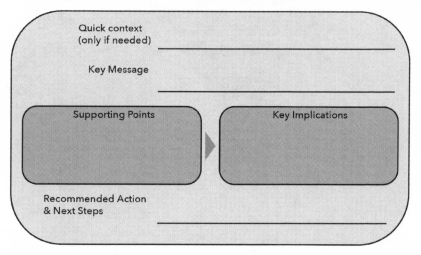

Quick context: Depending on whom you are talking to, you need to give a little bit of background to your audience so they are not lost. If it is someone who is highly familiar with an issue, like your boss, it could be as easy as "the purpose of this meeting is for me to explain our Q4 financial statement to you." For other audiences, you need to take a step back and provide a longer explanation. The important point is that you only give them as much context as they need, and then move on with your story.

Key message: This is where you deliver your main point concisely in two or three sentences. In my REI shopping excursion example, I would calmly state, "The kids and I have been in a car accident, but we are OK. Now let me tell you more about it."

Supporting points: These are the two to four main things that support or further explain your key message.

Key Implications: Implications lead the listener along in a way that helps show that you've done some thinking about your supporting points. Going over implications also helps prepare the listener for your final recommendation and next steps.

Recommended actions and next steps: You should rarely tell a story without having thought through what to do next. If you do this, say, to your boss, he will feel like you've just dropped a problem on his desk and that you want him to come up with a solution.

A Case Study

After I explain the framework to my trainees, I have them use it in a case in which Sean, an employee of a baby clothing company, has to give some bad news to his boss, Jessica. The situation is set up with this introduction:

Sean is a retail buyer for Babywear, Inc., a leading retailer of baby clothing, with 1,200 stores worldwide. He recently noticed that his business—baby pajamas—is down 12% on profit for the quarter compared to last year, even while sales have been flat. He notices this trend just as he receives a friendly note from his VP, Jessica, asking him to swing by her desk in one hour to give him an update on quarterly profit performance. He has one hour to prepare his thoughts...

Then I give them an example of a terrible response. Below is exactly the kind of response that Sean shouldn't give:

Hi Jessica, nice to see you. I've been looking at a lot of data. I just got off the phone with procurement and they were talking to me about commodities and that we've had a lot of challenges lately with cotton, which is a huge driver of our profit. I guess cotton prices are up 8% this year. They were saying that they haven't seen those kinds of trends since the 80s. Our profit is down 12% this quarter vs. last year. I didn't really expect to see that, but guess with these cotton prices...

Also, our biggest competitor, "Tots Threads," did some huge promotional discounts during the holidays of up to 25 percent off of most of their items, which forced us to do some price matching. And, in addition to cotton, our polyester prices are up 18% this year. Polyester goes into about 30% of our baby clothing, especially our premium lines, while cotton is about 50%. Procurement wasn't really sure what the future forecast looks like when I spoke with them but they have got to have some sort of forecasting model to predict these things. If our cotton prices don't come down, I think our profits could be quite suppressed for a while. And if "Tots Threads" continues these promotions, then we'll likely continue to engage in a pricing war with them in order to protect our market share. There is also an industry report that shows that, last quarter, consumers bought 6% less clothing at specialty baby clothes retailers this year, while at the same time, discount retailers are seeing a jump in 4% in their baby pajamas sales this year. I believe all this data answers your questions. I'm going to leave these reports with you so you can look them over as well. There is a ton more data in here that I haven't had a chance to look at yet, but I will.

This response, although horrible, includes the critical facts of what is going on. I then tell my trainees to pull out the facts in Sean's jumbled response, and reorganize them using the storytelling framework, like so:

Quick context	I'm here to give you an update on quarterly profit performance. I've done some analysis to talk about performance and key drivers. I'll walk you through that here in the next 15 minutes, and then we can talk about next steps
Key Message	Our profit is down 12% last quarter vs. a year ago driven by commodity prices, competitive activity, and customers shifting their baby item purchases to big-box retailers

Supporting Points / Drivers	Key Implications
1. Commodity Prices: cotton and polyester up 8% and 18% respectively 2. Competitive Promotions: Tots Threads holiday discounting by up to 25% caused us to price match 3. Mix shifting to big-box retailers: baby retailers down 6% while big big-box retailer baby sales +4%	1. Given that this is 80% of our cost inputs this would continue to have a material impact on our profit if these trends don't turn around 2. This poses the question: should we reevaluate our price-matching strategy if this continues? 3. Need to assess if this trend will continue

Recommended Action & Next Steps	1. Work with procurement to model out commodity prices 2. Conduct a price-elasticity study to see what would happen if we stopped price matching against competition 3. Put together a targeted direct mail program to get those that are switching to big-box retailers back to our stores

STORYTELLING RESPONSE

Once the story is fleshed out using the storytelling framework, it becomes much easier to structure a clear story. Here's an example of a strong response:

Hi Jessica, thanks for asking me to meet with you. You wanted to talk about why my profit is down this year by 12%, while my sales are flat versus a year ago. I've dug into the data and understand exactly what is going on. I want to explain that for you and talk about the action plan that is in place to improve the trends.

The 12% profit problem is a function of three drivers:

1. *Commodity prices have risen this year: Half of our problem, or six points of decline, can be attributed to the rise in commodity prices. Our two biggest inputs to baby jammies, cotton and polyester, have risen by 25% this year.*

2. *We have taken our prices down: In order to continue the same level of sales on our products, we have had to increase our sales at key times during the year. This is 25% of our problem.*

3. *We are seeing competition from discount retailers: This is a broad trend across our store. We know that our traffic is down and that many people are leaving our stores and shopping more at discount retail stores like Target and Wal-Mart. This is the other 25% of our problem.*

As next steps, there are several actions that we can take to rectify this situation

1. *Meet with procurement on this issue and ask them to look into ways to mitigate these costs going forward, including considering some alternative suppliers*

2. *Evaluate the efficiency of these programs and generate ideas on how to get those purchases back without having to put items on sale as much. These ideas may include better in-store signage to highlight the benefits of our products and ordering my merchandise so that we can sell more high-profit items.*

3. *Meet with buyers from other departments and we are putting together a plan to drive more people to our stores, including direct mail advertisements.*

I will be setting up a meeting with you next week, as I should have a firm recommendation by then on what to do. What questions or comments do you have for me?

Both the data-telling and storytelling responses in this case study include essentially the same information. Yet one is confusing and the other is clear. One casts doubt on the abilities of the teller, while the other one enhances the teller's credibility. These two responses demonstrate that storytelling is less about the facts themselves and more about how the facts are structured to build the credibility and push the agenda of the storyteller.

Reframing as a Storytelling Technique

Reframing is the art of recognizing an opposing point of view and then flipping it on its head in such a way that it works to your advantage. Highly persuasive storytellers use reframing as a way to get what they want. Reframing is the opposite of defensiveness. Defensiveness shows a complete disregard for an opposing point of view. Reframing, on the other hand, shows respect for the opposing point of view and the person presenting it. Defensiveness shows such a lack of confidence that it reduces a story's credibility, while reframing works with a calm confidence that enhances it. Defensiveness generally creates negativity and animosity, while reframing can break down barriers, build unity, and even create humor.

Good politicians are reframing masters. One classic example of reframing is how Ronald Regan, "The Great Communicator," responded to a tough question in the Reagan/Mondale Presidential debate of 1984[4]

> Moderator (addressing President Reagan): "You are already the oldest President in history, and some of your staff said that you were tired after your recent encounter with Mr. Mondale, I recall yet that President Kennedy who had to go with days on end with very little sleep during the Cuban Missile Crisis...is there any doubt in your mind, that you would be able to function in such circumstances?"
>
> President Reagan: "Not at all...and I want you to know also that I will not make age an issue of this campaign. I am not going to exploit for political purposes my opponent's youth and inexperience."

Quite an example of reframing! Not only did President Reagan disarm his opponent in a humorous way, but he also took a potential weakness—old age—and turned it into a fundamental strength—experience and wisdom.

---

4 Presidential Debate, Reagan vs. Mondale, 1984

One might dismiss this technique as being "quick-witted," or "able to think on your toes," but it is much more than that. This skill wins elections in politics and earns promotions in corporations. Opposition to your point of view will happen on a daily basis at your company. Your boss, your peers, and your employees will likely challenge what you are trying to accomplish. If you think you are wrong, admit it, but if you still believe in your point of view, then reframing is a much better alternative than getting defensive or simply caving in.

Reframing may seem awkward at first but, with practice and experience, it can become second nature. Using a reframing model process is broken down into three steps.

The first step is to consider the opposing challenge to your point of view. Rather than get defensive, take a deep breath and run the challenge through the reframing model. Let's use the Ronald Reagan debate example to demonstrate how this works.

1. **What is literally being said?** In this case, the debate moderator asked Reagan if he had any doubts about his ability to function on little sleep, given how old he is. Reagan could have simply answered, "No, I have no doubts that I could function under these circumstances," but he didn't. That is because he recognized that there was more to his question. Once Reagan understood what he was being asked, he was able to consider the next question.

2. **What is the bigger question that he is asking?** While the moderator was asking whether or not he could function with lack of sleep, what he was really asking is if the President thought he was too old to be President. Once this is understood, it opens up a whole new range of potential answers.

3. **Assuming the challenge is valid, what are the potential positives?** The claim, in this case, is true— President Reagan was going to be the oldest President in history! But while the moderator was insinuating that this is negative, there could be a whole host of positive implications as well, namely, experience, wisdom, and credibility. With this knowledge, the President essentially was able to turn a potential weakness and make it a strength.

The response: In essence, Reagan said "I have more experience than my opponent," albeit in a much more clever way.

This model can be used not only while debating issues in corporate meetings, but also through email, in writing business proposals, or when your boss challenges your assumptions on a project. Using the reframing model can become second nature with a little practice. Great storytellers use this technique so much that they don't even know they are using it. It just becomes a natural part of their leadership style. And it works!

In corporate America, there is a reframe for just about anything. Here are some examples;

Prompt: Jared is extremely stubborn and is never willing to change his point of view.

Reframe: Jared has a well-thought-out point of view and sticks to it, even in the face of opposition.

Prompt: Nancy is a class clown—no one can ever take her seriously.

Reframe: Nancy has the gift of bringing humor into every situation, which really brightens up our working environment.

Prompt: Our business is only a third of the size of our next competitor.

Reframe: When you look at our size vs. our competitor, we have significantly more runway for growth.

Stimulus: Nathan is not assertive enough—he never fights hard for his point of view.

Reframe: Nathan is highly collaborative and builds consensus among his team members.

Chapter Summary

- In today's corporate environment, data is everywhere
- Storytelling is better than data-telling. Data-tellers spit out facts and figures; storytellers synthesize the data in a story that drives action
- When telling stories with data, adhere to the following principles:
  1. Be biased
  2. Story first, data second
  3. Adapt to your audience
  4. Make the data relatable
  5. Keep it simple
- We like to tell stories this way:

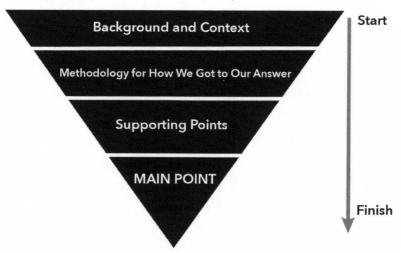

- Our co-workers, however, like to hear the opposite way

- When preparing a story at work, use the following framework to prepare:

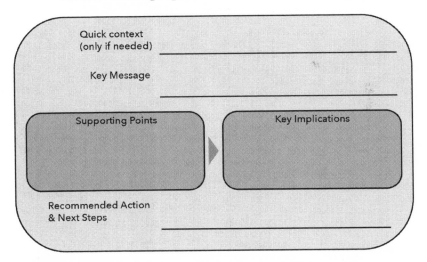

- Reframing is a technique used by highly persuasive storytellers
- To reframe, use the following questions, take a main point, and flip it upside down with a positive spin on it:

Quick context

I'm here to give you an update on quarterly profit performance. I've done some analysis to talk about performance and key drivers. I'll walk you through that here in the next 15 minutes, and then we can talk about next steps

Key Message

Our profit is down 12% last quarter vs. a year ago driven by commodity prices, competitive activity, and customers shifting their baby item purchases to big-box retailers

Supporting Points / Drivers

1. Commodity Prices: cotton and polyester up 8% and 18% respectively
2. Competitive Promotions: Tots Threads holiday discounting by up to 25% caused us to price match
3. Mix shifting to big-box retailers: baby retailers down 6% while big big-box retailer baby sales +4%

Key Implications

1. Given that this is 80% of our cost inputs this would continue to have a material impact on our profit if these trends don't turn around
2. This poses the question: should we reevaluate our price-matching strategy if this continues?
3. Need to assess if this trend will continue

Recommended Action & Next Steps

1. Work with procurement to model out commodity prices
2. Conduct a price-elasticity study to see what would happen if we stopped price matching against competition
3. Put together a targeted direct mail program to get those that are switching to big-box retailers back to our stores

5

SKILL #4: PRESENTING–OVER-PREPARE, OVER-DELIVER

*There are certain things in which mediocrity is not
to be endured, such as poetry, music, painting, and
public speaking.*

— Jean de la Bruyere

VIVIDLY REMEMBER THE FIRST TIME I FELT HUMILIATED AT
work. It was my second job out of college. I worked for a $3
billion consulting firm based in the Washington, D.C. area,
and my client was US Customs and Border Protection. My
company was helping Customs build software to better track
contraband coming across the border and to better collect du-
ties and fees on imports. My job was to make sure other US
agencies were informed and supportive of what we were doing.
In other words, I was a political cat-herder.

During my third week at work, I was asked to give a presentation to representatives from ten government agencies
about an enhanced website that we had launched. This website

helped these agencies stay connected with what we were doing at Customs, and we had given it a facelift to make it more user-friendly. My boss approached me about it a few days before the presentation to give me the assignment.

"We need to present the website to our stakeholders. I think you should go ahead and do it. You've been working on the website for a couple of weeks now and know it pretty well. It's a pretty slick site so I don't think anyone will have a problem with it. Just show them the website and how it works, and answer any questions that they have. You think you can handle that?"

I have no idea.

"Sure, happy to do it," I said with phony confidence.

Either my boss either wasn't aware of what I was up against or she really didn't like me, because the presentation did not go the way she had so euphemistically described it. In fact, the presentation brought to me a new-found respect for the term, "thrown to the wolves," because what I encountered in that 20-minute presentation was nothing short of a pack of growling, blood-thirsty government wolves bent on tearing me apart.

Two days after my boss's assignment, I sat in the US Treasury building in Washington, DC, and started my presentation. The first two minutes went fine, as I explained the purpose of the website and why we were improving it. But as I started to show the actual content of the website and how it worked, one government agency representative took issue with my work. "Why did you take out the data harmonization tab that was on the old website?" she asked.

I have no idea. I didn't build this thing.

"Um, I guess that part was left out because it was my under-standing that that portion of the work was already finished," I said.

I knew I had blurted out a terrible answer, so I was wincing inside, just waiting for someone to respond. And, of course, someone did.

"Well, let me educate you. It's far from finished!" said another agency representative.

The group erupted with laughter.

Ouch!

A few seconds later, the next person chimed in.

"Why did you change this button? It was fine the way it was."

"And what about having to change my password? Why can't I just keep my old password?"

"Honestly, the old website seemed easier to navigate."

And on and on it went. My presentation had officially "de-railed." The floodgates had been opened and anyone who didn't like the new website now had full permission to pile on in a completely safe environment. Even my co-workers who came to the presentation were powerless to stop it; all they could do was sit there and watch the train, now off its tracks, roll rapid-ly downhill. After a twenty-minute lashing by my audience, I thanked them for their time, took my things and walked to the train en route back to my office. I had failed.

When I returned to the office, I noticed people were look-ing at me differently, almost with sympathy, like I had recently fallen on the ground face-first and the scrapes on my cheeks and forehead were painful to look at. It had been only an hour or two since my presentation, but the news of my failure had

spread like wildfire. A few people even came by my desk to offer me words of encouragement and to tell me that they also
had royally screwed up early on in their careers, just like I had.
While the condolences were sincere, I got the general feeling
that everyone was glad this had happened to me, not them.

Fortunately, a team member who had more experience and
wisdom than I took pity on me. She said there would be another opportunity to present the website in the following month.
She worked with me on the presentation and forced me to
practice. Within a couple of weeks, this person had fundamentally changed the way I approached presenting. A month later,
I made the same presentation with the same group, and it went
off without a hitch

That experience taught me two vital lessons. First, never
underestimate the power that making a good (or bad) business presentation can have on one's career. The presentation
I gave in Washington, DC, that day was only twenty minutes,
but it took me a month to regain the trust and respect of my
team members. Second, it is not very hard to turn a poor presentation into a great presentation if you know what you are
doing. Looking back on that presentation, it is painfully obvious to me that my entire approach was wrong; yet my presentation was fixed by my co-worker with only a few hours of
extra work. There is no magic formula or code to crack. The
recipe for successful presentations is available to everyone.
And it's not that hard!

Under the Magnifying Glass

Presentations are extremely important for your career because they are extremely visible by others in your company. Early in your career, giving a presentation may be the only exposure you get to some key people in your organization. These people don't know or care about all the work that you do on a daily basis. They don't know or care whether or not you work extra hours; neither do they care whether or not you graduated college with honors. The only reference point they will have of you is the few minutes they listen to you while you present. From those few minutes, they will make a judgment about you. Totally unfair, but a reality nonetheless.

In this sense, presentations act as a magnifying glass. They make you highly visible for a short amount of time, allowing you the opportunity to either impress or disappoint. It doesn't matter what you did before you had the magnifying glass on you; that is all in the past. Now is the time to make sure they like what they are seeing.

Am I really saying that a thirty-minute presentation could have a drastic impact on your career at your company? Absolutely.

Why Most Presentations Are Mediocre

Delivering great business presentations is not hard. Yet as you read this book, there are thousands of people across the world, standing in conference rooms or auditoriums, giving dismal presentations. If you have worked in a big company for more than six months, you have witnessed this first-hand. This under-performance is not for lack of talent or potential, but rather for lack of preparation and effort. There are three primary reasons that employees don't put in the effort to be a good presenter.

1. **They don't see value in it**: These individuals do not believe presentations are important to their careers. They treat it as just another part of the job, putting it on par with generating a report, writing a brief, or hopping on a conference call. It never occurs to them that they are under the magnifying glass and that people are forming judgments about them as they present—judgments that could have a lasting effect on their career trajectories.

2. **They don't like presenting**: Many simply abhor presenting. This loathing is usually driven by fear. These people have either never learned how to give a presentation or have never had a successful experience. For these people, the whole process is overwhelming and fraught with anxiety, and so they prefer not to spend any time on it. In Chapter 2, I advocate investing in high-yield activities to propel your career, and part of a high-yield activity is enjoyment. Granted, if you hate making presentations, you may not be cut out for a career as a public speaker. But in order to succeed in a big company, you need to at least have a basic level of competence!

3. **They already think they are good at it:** This is especially common with less-experienced employees and is the very reason I bombed my presentation in Washington, DC. These individuals have grown up with teachers

and friends telling them that they are charismatic and good in front of audiences. Their over-confidence over-shadows their lack of understanding of what it takes to give a truly excellent presentation. They generally like making presentations and have "winged it" successfully in the past and assume that this is something they will never have to worry about. While these people have de-sire and potential, they overestimate their abilities and underestimate the challenge.

This chapter will help people in each group develop fantas-tic presentations. For Group 1, those who don't think it mat-ters, you will see the value of putting more effort into your presentations. It is not hard and a little extra effort can bring about drastic improvement. For Group 2, those who hate or fear giving presentations, I will eliminate any uncertainty about what it takes to give a great presentation. By going step-by-step through the preparation, delivery, and aftermath, the mystery underneath the black box will be gone, and hopefully the anxiety along with it. For those in Group 3, I will demon-strate that excellent presentations require more than natu-ral energy and a quick tongue. Charisma and an affinity for speaking show potential, but they do not equate to excellence. That can only be attained through learning, preparation, and practice. Just as a dancer with incredible rhythm and flex-ibility needs to learn and practice the steps to the waltz, so too you—even with all your energy and charisma—need to learn and practice the principles of good presenting in order to reach your potential.

There are three critical phases of great presentations: preparation, delivery, and aftermath. Each must be learned, internalized and practiced to achieve optimal success.

The Six Steps of Preparation

Preparation is by far the most important part of your presentation. Everyone, from newly minted employees to experienced executives, can sniff out an unprepared presentation within the first couple of minutes. While I am a proponent of "fake it 'til you make it," in some circumstances, a presentation is not the time to wing it. There is simply no substitute for taking the time for good preparation and practice. Here are the key elements to making sure you are prepared.

STEP ONE: KNOW YOUR AUDIENCE

During my first few years working as a marketing manager, my bosses beat into me a simple mantra: *Start with the consumer.* The meaning of this phrase is that when businesses consider offering new products or services, they must first understand who they are offering them to. While this may sound simple, businesses break this basic rule over and over again as they fall in love with technologies and scramble to find consumers to buy them. Many times, the products are of very good quality. The problem is that the makers of these products did not understand their audience. (For a small sample of examples, run a Google search on Crystal Pepsi, The Segway PT, and Harley Davidson Perfume.)

Starting with your consumer applies in business presentations. Regardless of the quality of the content you present, if it is not tailored to meet the needs of your audience, it will fall flat. Knowing your audience can ensure that you deliver your content in a way that is relevant and engaging to them.

When asked to give a presentation, you should ask yourself the following questions to better understand your audience:

- **Who am I presenting to?** Get the basics, like the number of people in attendance, their ages, genders, and how they fit into the hierarchy of their organization.

- **How familiar are they with the subject?** You want to know their level of expertise because it will drastically influence how deeply and broadly you go into a subject. Presenting about finance to a group of elementary students will take a much different direction than if you were to present to a group of money managers.

- **Why are they attending the presentation?** Find out if this is voluntary or a mandatory meeting for them. This will help you gauge their true interest and engagement in the subject.

- **Is there anyone in my audience that I should watch out for?** This question helps you understand whether there is someone in your presentation that can trip you up. For example, suppose you are making a presentation about effective selling to a group of life insurance agents. Will there be a thirty-year veteran of the industry in the crowd who has no problem interrupting you to assert his opinion? This person could be your best friend during the presentation or he could completely throw you off and derail you. Either way, knowing that he is there will help you develop a strategy.

- **Is there anyone in the audience that can be my advocate?** Is there someone in the audience who commands credibility over other members of the audience? Think about ways they can help you. Perhaps they can share a story during the presentation or give you an endorsement before you present.

- **What does my audience really want?** If you can understand what's in it for them, you can craft your presentation accordingly. Are they there to be trained, educated, entertained, or a combination of all three?

STEP TWO: DEVELOP A FOCUSED OBJECTIVE

Before you begin creating your content, focus your presentation by articulating your objective. That may sound simple, but can you remember the last time you heard a presentation that had a crystal clear objective?

Do not try to accomplish too much by creating multiple objectives. Most presenters try to do this and wind up delivering diluted and unmemorable content. A good rule of thumb is to assume your audience will only listen to about fifty percent of your presentation, and only remember about ten percent. The reality is that if your audience remembers your key message a few days after your presentation, you have done well. If they actually do something different as a result of your presentation, you have done excellently. The more clear and focused your objective, the better chance you have that your audience will remember and act on what you said.

As a tool to help you focus your objective, use the following objective statement: "The purpose of my presentation is to get {fill in the blank} to do {fill in the blank} by showing them {fill in the blank}." This will ensure that your objective is focused and tight because it describes exactly what you are trying to accomplish and how you are trying to accomplish it. An objective statement will help you turn a good objective into a great objective. Here are some examples of a perfectly fine objective turned great through this tool:

Average Objective: Help the tech support employees better understand customer service

Great Objective: Inspire the tech support employees to achieve excellence in customer service by showing them the benefit of powerful customer service principles

Average Objective: Teach high school kids about the dangers of drug use

Great Objective: Motivate high school students to never use drugs by showing them the horrible consequences of using drugs.

Average Objective: Tell the members of my church congregation about the service trip to Guatemala this summer

Great Objective: Persuade 25% of my congregation to sign up for the service trip to Guatemala by sharing emotional and inspiring stories of last year's trip.

STEP THREE: CREATE THE STRUCTURE OF YOUR CONTENT

Once you know your audience and have a clear objective, you are ready to start creating your content. Here are the guiding principles to create your content:

- **Develop a unique title:** Don't wait until you start your presentation to capture your audience's attention;

start that immediately with a great title. For example, a presentation about airplane safety could simply read "airplane safety procedures," but wouldn't it be better if it said, "the five things that will save your life on an airplane." The first one sounds like a snoozer; the second sounds like it may save my life someday.

- **Use variation:** Entertainment and engagement come first. If you can't keep them interested, you'll never be able to teach them anything, much less inspire them to action. To achieve this, consider using a variety of presentation methods in your presentation. These include personal stories, questions to the audience, pictures, charts and graphs, music, short film clips, and relevant quotes.

- **Put PowerPoint in its place:** How many presentations have you been to where the presenter simply puts verbose PowerPoint slides on a projector and then proceeds to read every single word on each slide? It happens all the time! While PowerPoint—or some other form of presentation software—can enhance your presentation, it should never drive it. Your presentation is all about you, and your content should be so good that you could deliver it without the crutch of PowerPoint and still have a successful presentation. If you must use PowerPoint:
  - Use a lot of pictures
  - Use few words
  - Use really, really large font
  - Give every slide a key point that is easy to understand and builds on your objective
  - Use simple charts that can be easily explained

You don't have to spell it all out for your audience on a PowerPoint slide. They don't want to read your presentation, and they certainly don't want to hear you read it. Make your slides work together with what you say to deliver the complete package. Some of the best presentations that I have seen are simply images, with people talking over them. It's possible to have a great presentation with zero words!

STEP FOUR: GUT-CHECK YOUR CONTENT FOR SIMPLICITY

Your presentation will be excellent only when every member of your audience understands and engages with your content. Never assume that your audience will just "get it." Cater to the lowest common denominator by asking yourself, "Will the dumbest person in the audience get this?" One way to make sure everyone gets your presentation it is to have someone review it who has no background on the subject.

STEP FIVE: PRE-SELL TO THE KEY STAKEHOLDERS

My friend, Jacob, works in the corporate office of a large US railroad. He related a story to me about a presentation he delivered:

> I had prepared a presentation for the executive committee. My content was really good. I'd worked on it for a long time and did a good job of finding facts to support my message, having a clear underlying story, and then a clear call to action. I was ready to present.
>
> I had my first PowerPoint slide up on the screen when the executive came in the room. The slide was the intro-

ductory slide and had a picture of a locomotive carrying coal. He took one look at the first slide and said, "Why the "$*%$ is there a coal train on that slide?" Why is it not an intermodal train?" (Intermodal trains are those that carry freight that can be carried on rail, truck, or ocean carrier.)

This presentation was for an executive in the Intermodal Department. Now I personally don't really care about the picture on the first slide of my presentations and I didn't think others would care either...but I was wrong. I set the presentation up poorly because he didn't like my opening slide. This was the first time he had seen it.

Jacob's story illustrates that failing to show your work to key people *before* you make your presentation means the risk of derailment *during* your presentation. Business executives don't like surprises when the stakes are high—especially negative ones. Recall that, in business, everyone wants to look good in front of their co-workers and boss, and when you surprise people in presentations, it's like backing tigers into a corner.

It is difficult to know which pieces of information will surprise people in your presentation, but here are some clues that your presentation may get some people uncomfortable:

- When you are forecasting numbers that could lead to commitments. For example, you could be framing up an estimated sales forecast for a new product that the salesperson in the audience will eventually be asked to deliver.
- When your boss is attending.

- When your boss's boss is attending.
- When key people in other departments are attending.
- When you are trying to get people to change behavior from the way things have always been done.
- When you are showing poor business results from either your department or a department in which people are attending the meeting.

Probably the biggest mistake I made in my failed presentation in Washington was not pre-selling my presentation to key stakeholders. The problem that got me derailed in my presentation was relatively easy to prevent, but I didn't recognize it until it was too late. I was completely blind-sided and caught off guard.

Pre-selling is an easy yet often forgotten step. Pressure and deadlines usually get in the way. In addition, it's human nature to want your work to be perfect before you show it. But it's better to get a presentation in front of people early to know if you are on the right track—even if it's not 100% complete.

Pre-selling has the following benefits:

1. It allows you to filter out any major mistakes or political oversights that you may have made ahead of the final presentation so that there are no surprises.
2. It shows people that you are willing to take their feedback into consideration before presenting it.
3. It usually gets your presentation in a better place because you have done your homework.

Sometimes you will not have the opportunity to show your presentation to everyone in your audience. You may not know everyone in your audience, or you may not have time, or it may just not be practical. In this case, you need to take at least a few minutes and try to anticipate the questions that you may be asked. Walk through each of your key talking points along with your visual aids, and ask yourself, "What would someone in a different department ask about this slide?" This will help you prepare answers in your head before the questions are asked and increase the likelihood that you will give good answers.

STEP SIX: PRACTICE, PRACTICE, PRACTICE...AND THEN PRACTICE SOME MORE

The final step in your preparation is to practice until there is no doubt that you will be successful. Practice until you have nearly memorized your talking points. Practice until you know that even if the electricity went out and you had to deliver your presentation by candlelight without any sort of electronic assistance, you could still deliver it well.

With sufficient practice comes sufficient confidence. There is a difference between having pre-presentation jitters, and just being plain scared that you've underprepared. Practice eradicates fear.

Delivery

You now understand your audience. You have created and gut-checked your content. You have presold your presentation to those that matter. Finally, you have practiced until you are sick of your presentation. It is now time to stand and deliver!

Here are the keys to excellent delivery.

START STRONG

Do not underestimate how important it is to start your presentation strong. Arrive early so that you can start creating positive feelings by greeting your audience with a smile and/or a handshake, if possible, when they enter the room. It is also wise to make sure that all your technological aids are working correctly. How many times have you started a business meeting and the presenter says something like "Welcome, we are having some technical difficulties, so please stand by. I apologize for the delay." Do you really want to start off your presentation with an apology?

People will remember the first and last part of your presentation the most, so get started off right. Make sure that the first words you utter set the tone for an engaging professional experience. So many presenters start off with some terrible first words:

Opening Statement: *Sorry I'm late everyone. I appreciate your patience.*

Audience Interpretation: *To prove that I'm not a punctual person, I didn't even show up to my own presentation on time!*

Opening Statement: *I'm feeling pretty nervous right now, so hopefully I don't faint up here.*

Audience Interpretation: *I am going to act nervous through the whole presentation and, as a result, you are going to feel anxious and on edge the entire time.*

Opening Statement: *I really hate public speaking, so I'm hoping I can get through this.*

Audience Interpretation: *This is going to suck.*

Opening Statement: *I just got the assignment to present a few hours ago, so I haven't really had time to prepare.*

Audience Interpretation: *This presentation is going to be an all-around disappointment, so I might as well start making excuses immediately.*

Opening Statement: *This probably won't take the total scheduled time, so you will be able to get some time back.*

Audience Interpretation*: I really shouldn't have scheduled this much time with you since I knew from the outset that my presentation won't take as long as I've scheduled.*

Opening Statement: *When asked to make this presentation, my first thought was....*

Audience Interpretation*: I'm going to try the classic ice-breaker and talk about what I was thinking when I was asked to present, even though it is unrelated to my content and a complete throw-away.*

Opening Statement: *We are going to start just a few minutes late today because we are just experiencing some technical difficulties with the projector.*

Translation: *I didn't take the time before the presentation to ensure everything was ready.*

You can still recover from a poor opening start to a presentation, but why start a presentation in a hole? Why not start out strong? There are many easy ways to start a presentation that help build confidence and credibility from the get-go. For example, suppose you are giving a presentation about globalization. Here are some viable ways that you could start:

Option 1: Lay out the presentation in one sentence: "Today I will speak with you about globalization—specifically, how it affects the textile, steel and agriculture industries."

Option 2: Start with a story: "I remember the first time I realized all my clothing was made in other countries...."

Option 3: Start off with compelling facts: "When I was born 35 years ago, 30% of all the textiles sold in the US were made overseas. Today, 85% of textiles are made overseas."

Everyone you are presenting to is hoping that they are in for an entertaining and educational experience. Give them that reassurance by opening your presentation strong. The old adage, "You never get a second chance to make a first impression," applies here. Your audience is not likely to give you very much time before they decide in their minds whether to listen to a credible and interesting person, or whether they should plan their escape.

Entertainment is Critical: There is no such thing as a captive audience. Throughout your whole presentation, you are in a cutthroat competition for your audience's attention. Your competitor is everyone's mobile phone—and what a fierce competitor it is. Here is the critical question to ask yourself when practicing your presentation: Would my audience prefer to watch me present over watching a funny cat video online or playing solitaire electronically? If the answer is "No," you are in trouble.

DRESS NOT TO IMPRESS

The theories of the how to dress for a business presentation seem infinite: Dress slightly better than your audience so they know that you mean business; dress slightly worse than your audience to disarm them; don't dress too fancy so as to come off as arrogant; don't dress too casual because people won't take you seriously; if you work in banking, dress in a suit; if you are in tech, use a black turtleneck and sneakers; never wear white; never wear black; never wear pink. This list is endless!

So how should you dress for a business presentation? The answer to this question can be answered through a quick mental exercise. Think of a great presentation that you have heard recently. It could be at work, school, church, or any other venue with a formal presenter. Then list five things made it a great presentation, in order of importance.

Now, if your list is anything like mine, the presenter's manner of dress did not make the list. More important was that the content was interesting and relevant, the speaker was engaging and told great stories, and that you learned something useful. The way someone dresses just doesn't matter that much.

Unless dress is specifically relevant to your subject, (like a clown act or weight-lifting demonstration), the way you are dressed shouldn't matter. Your goal, then, is quite counterintuitive: You should dress so as to make no impression at all. In fact, you want people to forget about how you look and lose themselves in the presentation content.

The best way to "dress not to impress" is to make sure what you are wearing doesn't pull focus away from your presentation. Find out how everyone else will be dressed, and match the general standards of the day, not wearing anything that will specifically draw attention away from your content.

END STRONG—AND ON TIME!

Suppose there are ten minutes left of your hour-long presentation and you are only halfway through your content. Perhaps your audience has asked more questions than you anticipated, or maybe you didn't put in enough time practicing and miscalculated how long it would take to get through your content. If you are an inexperienced presenter, you will likely employ one of two tactics, both of which will de-value your presentation.

The first tactic is to keep plowing through our content at the same pace, and thus go over your time limit. Bad idea! In social life, being late is excusable and occasionally "fashionable." But in big companies, tardiness is flat-out rude.

The second thing you may do is speed up your presentation so as to get through all of your content in a condensed amount of time. After all, you spent so much time preparing the content; it would be a crying shame not to deliver, right? Wrong! This tactic is another bad idea. If you do this, the audience will easily pick up that you are hurrying your content and you won't be able to drive your main point home.

The best way to handle this situation is to cut your content short. Skip it. Clam it. Put a fork in it—you get it. Nobody else knows that you are skipping content but you, so plan ahead and know which pieces of your presentation you can cut and how you can still smoothly transition to your conclusion.

That's how you end on time, which is the first step to making sure you end strong. The next step is to understand how you structure your conclusion. Don't use a throw-away ending like "so that's the end," or "thank you for your time," or "and with that, I'll be happy to take any of your questions." You have a golden opportunity to finish strong; don't throw it away! Consider all the options you have to choose from. You can choose to:

1. Summarize your presentation in a compelling way
2. Return to a story that you started with, now with added insight
3. Tell a new, but applicable, story
4. Give a final quote
5. Ask a provocative or rhetorical question to your audience

People remember the beginning and end of presentations, so go out with a bang!

Followup and Feedback

The third and final phase of creating a great presentation is the most under-utilized of all. This is the phase where you tie up loose ends and, more importantly, learn how to improve for your next presentation. Many presenters spend time to prepare and deliver but do not complete this final step. Yet those who are serious about improvement will make it this far.

INSTALLING FEEDBACK SYSTEMS

I once observed a highly respected executive give what I thought was a masterful thirty-minute presentation on his billion-dollar business. He was well-prepared and delivered what I thought was a remarkable presentation. After the presentation, I was sitting at my desk when I heard him walking back to his office with another co-worker. The co-worker had a note-pad with notes on it. He was known as an honest and candid person, someone who would give you honest feedback if asked. "Come give me your notes," I heard the executive say. Then they both entered the office and shut the door.

This executive had done something that executives rarely do. He had put a feedback system into place. He had asked someone to take notes during the presentation and critique him afterward. There are multiple ways to do this, but here are some examples:

- Do surveys—quick online surveys are free and quick, and can provide valuable feedback. I do this for many of my own trainings.
- Schedule a private meeting with your boss or peers to ask what you could have done better.
- Videotape your presentation so you can view or listen to your performance afterward.

Chapter Summary

- Like it or not, business presentations have a magnifying effect on your career, either good or bad.

- Most presentations are mediocre for one of three reasons:
  - People don't understand the importance for their careers.
  - People hate or fear presenting.
  - People mistakenly think they are already great presenters.

- Anyone can deliver a great presentation, as long as they are willing to pay the preparation price.

- There are six steps to preparing a great presentation:
  - Know your audience by asking critical questions about them.
  - Develop a focused objective.
  - Create content that includes a unique title and varied teaching methods, and that puts PowerPoint in its place.
  - Gut-check your content for simplicity.
  - Pre-sell your presentation to key stakeholders.
  - Practice, practice, and, um, practice.

- Some tips for great delivery include:
  - Start out with a strong opening statement.
  - Dress NOT to impress.
  - End with a bang—and on time!

- After your presentation is complete, get feedback about your performance through surveys, by videotaping yourself, or by asking a trusted co-worker how you can improve.

6

SKILL #5: PERSUADING–MAKE THOSE WHO DON'T WORK FOR YOU... WORK FOR YOU

Leadership: The art of getting someone else to do something you want done because they want to do it."
— Dwight Eisenhower

"THERE'S YOUR PAYCHECK, SAM!" SHOUTED MY BOSS, AS HE pointed to a food production line. I was in western Iowa, touring the manufacturing plant that produced the frozen meals that I marketed. The environment inside the plant was noisy, hot, smelly, and frenetic. Employees moved up and down the floor continuously, some pushing large tubs filled with ingredients, others monitoring the machinery, and still others barking orders at line workers. Conveyor belts carried chicken, noodles, and vegetables into dispensers that dropped them into trays and eventually packed them inside cartons and cases. Vigilant, hair-netted line workers checked to make sure there were no defects in the meals that were whizzing by at a clip of over one hundred units per minute. Employees driving forklifts hauled pallets of cases back to a giant blast freezer for storage, then quickly returned to pick up more pallets. The whole ordeal was truly remarkable. I had never seen anything like it.

Despite all the activity going on around me in the plant, my mind tuned it out after my boss' comment. *There's your paycheck, Sam.* It played over and over in my head. He was right. Without that production line and processes and people that accompanied it, I wouldn't have a product to sell. All the machinery, line laborers, engineers, and administrative staff were helping to build something that enabled me to get paid. Should I have attempted to build all that on my own, it would have taken me more than a lifetime. To some degree, my success depended on them.

A fundamental part of a long and prosperous career at a big company is the ability to get things done, and that involves enlisting the help of others. Why? Because today's business world is far too complex for one individual to handle alone. People in corporations fundamentally need one another to be successful.

Consider a basic car tire. Here's a short list of the experts needed to produce and sell it:

- Procurement specialist: purchases the materials that make up the tire
- Product engineer: designs the tire to certain specifications
- Manufacturing personnel: produces the product. Or, if the company outsources its tire production, then it needs experts to select and manage the outsourced company.
- Marketing manager: Creates consumer demand for the products

- Sales manager: Sells the tire into the proper distribution channels
- Accounting and/or finance manager: Keeps track of the money, and likely helps evaluate and set correct pricing
- Legal: Ensures the company meets all legal requirements and protects against lawsuits
- Project manager: Keeps track of all the moving parts and the timeline
- Human resources manager: Attempts to keep all employees happily compensated and engaged at work (the key word here is "attempts")
- IT specialist: Manages the technology you use to get the work done
- Administrative assistant: The catch-all for all other details

This list barely scratches the surface. Within each of the functions mentioned above, there are multiple specialties. It is impossible to expect one person alone to handle these tasks at a large corporation. Only multiple experts working together can produce and sell a high-quality tire at a competitive market price.

This is not to say that there is no place for individual work in an organization—clearly, you should seek to make an individual contribution in your area of expertise. But if you rely solely on your individual work, you will miss the opportunity to have your impact magnified through others.

Formal education does not teach this. Rather, it focuses squarely on the individual. Tests are taken alone in school. Homework is completed alone. Grades are given out according to one's personal mastery of a subject. Having someone else complete a portion of your homework is considered cheating.

Not so in business. In fact, nearly everything that gets done at a large company today is the result of several experts working together. Enlisting others at your company in your cause is far from cheating—it's leadership! And it's a vital skill.

Leadership in corporations is defined as getting others to do their best work for you. Great leaders become great because of their ability to influence others, not because of their ability to complete functional tasks. Jack Welch, Henry Ford, Steve Jobs, and other great corporate leaders all had twenty-four hours in a day, just like you and me. It's laughable to think they achieved their success only by themselves. In truth, they had many smart and capable people helping them. They simply had a remarkable ability to magnify their visions through others.

Persuasion over Power

There are two influence methods employed by leaders at big companies, and they are drastically different from one another. Power—the first method—is an option available to you if you have a lot of people reporting to you or a very important title at your company. But unless you are high up in your company, power tactics will not work. In fact, using power tactics will often have the opposite effect on those you work with than what you intended. Many times, you will create distrust and incite frustration and anger from your co-workers. For example, if you have a disagreement with a co-worker and you both have valid concerns, a classic power play is to go directly to the co-worker's boss in order to get your way. The assumption with this strategy is that this person's boss will then compel the person to do what you've asked, even though he or she has already clearly demonstrated that they don't want to do it. In this case, even if you get what you want, you have sabotaged your credibility with your co-worker. Good luck getting that person to trust you in the future.

Even senior executives, who carry plenty of weight in big companies by virtue of their titles, will get only so far by using those titles. They may get what they want in the short term but employees are obeying not out of a genuine motivation, only for self-preservation. And they are not happy about it; no one wants to work in an environment where they feel forced to do things they don't want to do.

Employees without a powerful title but who seek to compel with power, often use other people's titles to get things done—also known as "name-dropping." "John (you know, the VICE-PRESIDENT), asked me to get this done," or, "Your boss asked me to tell you..." are common opening statements used with this tactic. While you may get some short-term things accomplished this way, name-dropping will erode trust over the long term. Doing something simply because someone higher than you wants it done is a nod to power, not logic.

Despite the attractiveness of using power to get your way, there is a second, more effective method to get people to help you: persuasion. This method differs from power in nearly every way. The table below demonstrates a few of those differences.

Influence Through Power	Influence Through Persuasion
Tell people what to do by dropping names	Convince people what needs to be done with logic
Establish transactional relationships with others	Establish personal relationship with others
Appeal to authority	Appeal to the vision or cause
Use title	Use personal influencing skills
Give orders	Ask questions and make suggestions
Work gets done because powerful person wants it done	Work gets done because workers want to do it
Decision rights are centralized to leader	Decision rights are decentralized to employees
Comfortable only when in control	Comfortable with being vulnerable

Granted, power is easier to use than persuasion. It requires less patience. It may enable you to get more done in the short term. But here is the great irony of using power in big companies: the more you use it, the less of it you have. Thus, choose carefully when to use a power card. You don't have an unlimited supply of them.

With persuasion, on the other hand, you may not get what you want every time. To persuade, you must work within the parameters of the person's ability to reason and to choose. This can often test your patience and willpower, but it will ultimately create stronger results, build better business relationships, and create a stronger reputation for you as a leader.

This is not to say that power should never be used. Indeed, there are rare occasions that power or authority should be used over persuasion. For example, when safety—for either customer or employee—is at risk and correction is required immediately, power can be used to prevent disaster. There is no time to persuade in these cases. But most issues are not that urgent in corporate life. Persuasion tactics should be your "go-to" if you want the right kind of people to do the right kinds of things for you.

Persuasion Principle #1: Get Co-Workers to Genuinely Like You

Abraham Lincoln said: "If you would win a man to your cause, first convince them that you are his sincere friend."[5] Getting others to like you is the first and most fundamental tactic to use in persuading others. It is the gateway that opens ups all other persuasion tactics. When people like you, there is a greater chance they will help you when you need it. They will be more forgiving when you make mistakes, more likely to give you praise when you succeed, and more willing to help you when you are in a pinch.

The good news is that this tactic is incredibly easy to implement. It requires no skill—just action. I have found the following six suggestions to be very effective in getting others to like you:

1. **Build the relationship BEFORE you need something**: Invest the time to get to know your co-workers on a personal level. Walk over to a co-worker's desk and talk with them for a while and say nothing about business. You'll be surprised how fast you can build a

---

5 Abraham Lincoln address to the Washington Temperance Society, Feb 22, 1842

relationship in little time. And, you will be surprised at their willingness to help when you need something.

2. **Perform random acts of kindness:** Suppose you find out that a co-worker is struggling with a business problem. Perhaps he is struggling with PowerPoint. Show him a few tricks to fix it. Or maybe they need someone to listen to them vent. Invest fifteen minutes in lending him your ear. My personal favorite act lately is to pay for someone else's lunch in the company cafeteria. (I've probably lost a few hundred dollars doing this over the years, but favors I get in return are worth every penny!) These acts communicate "I like you" to the recipient. Random acts of kindness can be very small, yet they matter to the person receiving it. The magic is in their authenticity. They can't be contrived or geared to immediately get something in return. Just give, and give it with no strings attached.

Kindness has a way of flowing back to people who give it out. I once bought a t-shirt for a co-worker with a message on it that I knew had significance for him. It was a genuine gift that I knew he would enjoy, and I did it because I liked him. It took me ten minutes and cost me fifteen dollars but my relationship with that person was changed forever.

1. **Handwrite thank-you notes**: In today's digital age, it is so easy to shoot off a quick text or email thanking someone for something. This is not a bad thing in itself but taking the time to write a handwritten note shows more effort.

2. **Send a complimentary note to their boss:** Who doesn't like to look good in front of their boss? This can really go a long way toward building positive momentum with your co-workers.

3. **Ask for help:** This sounds counterintuitive. One should, theoretically, seek to give help—not take it—in order to be liked, but asking for help is one of the best ways to build rapport with someone else. It demonstrates authenticity and vulnerability. People can relate to vulnerability because everyone is vulnerable to some degree. Showing vulnerability by asking for help enables others to let down their guard when they are around you and feel good about themselves in the process. And then when they do help you—make sure you genuinely thank them for their assistance.

4. **Demonstrate loyalty:** When something goes wrong on a project, never disparage or belittle your team members in front of others—especially those higher up in the organization. If needed, take corrective action with a team member in person, but always ensure them of your loyalty.

These suggestions may seem overly obvious. They are. But consider your own habits. Do you consistently perform acts of kindness for co-workers or do you let the demands of the business get in the way? Do you see others in your organization doing these things on a regular basis? The problem with these ideas is not that they are overly-simple, but that they are rarely used.

This is all upside for you if you take advantage. There are no special skills required, just action. Try them out and reap the rewards. Then let other people wonder why everyone wants to work with and help you before anyone else.

Persuasion Principle #2: Establish Respect

I suppose everyone wants to be liked AND respected at the same time. For the most part, this is fully possible and should be sought after. Yet, when faced with the choice between being liked and being respected in business, you must choose to be respected. If you are respected and not liked, you can still get things done through others, although it may be a little unpleasant at times. On the other hand, if you are liked but not respected, you will be like a cute little kid at the neighborhood BBQ whom everyone dotes on but nobody listens to. Without respect, you will have little ability to influence and persuade.

Persuasion Principle #3: Be Consistent

The key to garnering respect among your co-workers is consistency. Consistency is saying what you'll do, and then doing what you say—then expecting the same from other people. It's about binding yourself to certain principles, and then not deviating from them.

My friend, John, has a very strong-willed child named Luke. Kyle and his wife, Mary, noticed his strong will when he was about 2 or 3, as he would frequently try their patience—more so than the average 2- or 3-year-old. One day, Mary called Kyle after a play group, where she was forced to leave out of desperation, because Luke was completely out of control, hitting other kids such that the mothers were giving her dirty looks. Through her tears she said, "I felt so embarrassed. I don't know what to do with him." They would get frustrated and threaten him with "time out," or take away toys, but Luke would eventually wear them down over time and find a way out of his consequences. They didn't know what else to do but hope he would grow out of it.

Then the most amazing thing happened. Luke's preschool teacher told John and Mary that Luke had been having problems in school getting along with the other children. His strong will made him very difficult to control when he was upset. It was beginning to disrupt and cause problems in class. They recommended a good counselor that might be able to help. Not having any better solutions, they decided to give it a try. Here is Mary's account:

> When we arrived at the counselor's office, she sat Luke down and told him that he could play with only certain toys while she and I talked. Then she explained to him that if he disobeyed and played with toys that were not allowed, that she was going to put him in "time out" on the chair.
>
> Luke agreed, and the counselor started talking with me. Not a couple of minutes had passed, and Luke started to play with the toys that were prohibited. The counselor picked Luke up, sat him on the chair, and told him, "I told you that you weren't supposed to play with those toys. You will now sit in time out in this chair until I say you can get out." Luke flipped out. He screamed and screamed. He yelled out, "you are the worst doctor ever!" He pleaded for me to help him. I have to admit, I felt bad for him and started to tear up a little

bit. Luke was my son, and he knew how to tug on my heart-strings. Yet all the while, the counselor looked at me calmly and assured me that this needed to be done.

After what seemed like an hour, Luke finally began to calm down, but his attitude stayed rotten. Because of this attitude, he got to stay in time out until he shaped up. Finally, toward the end of the appointment, Luke realized that time out was not worth it, and slowly started showing good behavior and respect.

That first appointment with the counselor was the beginning of a huge change for Kyle and me. Through this and subsequent appointments, she taught us the power of consistency. In truth, there was nothing inherently wrong with Luke. He, like many children, had his own way of thinking. What he craved was someone in the home to lead with consistency. We needed to prove to him that we were worthy of his obedience. So, in the weeks and months ahead, we diligently kept our promises. We were careful about which warnings we issued, but we always delivered on our promised consequences. It was very hard. It required persistence and endurance. But Luke eventually got the message that we meant business. His behavior gradually improved and by the next year he went into kindergarten a well-behaved boy, ready to learn and grow.

Luke's story applies to how business relationships should be managed. If we wish to have the respect of others, we must earn it by being consistent. We do this by ensuring that our words and actions are in harmony. When people recognize the congruence between what we say and what we do, respect inevitably follows.

Persuasion Principle #4: Ask for Commitments

Each of your co-workers desires to be consistent; no one wants to be seen as undependable or as a flake. In business, you must expect consistency from others. One way to ensure consistency in others is by using a basic technique of asking questions and following up. I include this simple technique because I am shocked by how underutilized it is in business. Your co-workers have a desire to be consistent as well and you can use this to your advantage.

Melanie was a co-worker of mine who was extremely smart, talented, and kind. Yet Melanie was periodically frustrated with her team members.

"I just don't understand why other teammates don't listen to me," she would say. "How many times do I have to tell people what to do? It's almost as if people are just deliberately ignoring me!"

Melanie could be quite persuasive when trying to get others to help her. She gave great presentations with strong logic of why things should be done. She even mentioned how grateful she was in advance for the work that they were going to do. But she failed to do one very simple thing: *Ask* them for direct commitment.

For whatever reason (unwillingness to appear confrontational or condescending, perhaps) she would never commit people to completing tasks. She simply *assumed* that they would do it. Yet in a corporate environment, where human resources are scarce, there is no room for assumption. When team members have several competing priorities, not to mention their own bosses to please, one must be very direct. No fanfare needed—a simple question does the job.

EXAMPLE:

You are a product manager and need Jeremy, a finance expert, to run a scenario for you by tomorrow at noon to help you understand how you should price a new product. Jeremy is familiar with the project and has the ability to complete this task. In this case, there are two methods you can use to get this done.

Option 1: "Melanie's" method: "Jeremy, I'm looking to have a financial analysis done soon. Once we get it, it will really help us understand how we should price our products. And if we get it right, it will be a fantastic product launch that could completely change the game for our business! So thanks for your help. Let's get it done!"

Option 2: Question Method: Jeremy, will you please run a financial analysis to help me determine pricing of our new product by tomorrow at noon?

The first option is certainly more exciting. It may be even more motivating. But after this exchange, you still don't know whether or not Jeremy will complete his requested task.

The second option is less fancy, but you can be sure that you will walk away knowing where you stand. If he says "Yes," then you have succeeded. If he says "No," then at least you know you have a problem—which is more than you would have known with Option 1.

The beauty of a question is that it makes followup extremely easy. For example, if the committed due date comes and Jeremy hasn't completed his task, there is no need to get frustrated; simply approach Jeremy and say the following: "Hi Jeremy, yesterday you kindly agreed to complete a financial analysis by noon today. It's noon now; do you have it?"

So many people in the business world never do this because it makes them feel uncomfortable. They don't want to appear pushy, condescending, or confrontational. They prefer to stew about it in silence until it finally festers enough to where they vent about it to other people or even start to treat Jeremy differently. This passive-aggressive approach gets nothing done and causes elevated blood pressure unnecessarily.

Following up on a question is remarkably easy. There is no yelling, frustration, or cajoling. Someone has made a commitment to you; now let him explain why he is not delivering on it.

Principle #5: Find Mentors

I was once asked to give a letter of recommendation for a business associate. He was a friend, but not a close one at the time. Yet something happened during the letter-writing process that I did not expect. While writing, I found myself remembering all the positive associations that I had had with him. I wound up writing a strong letter of recommendation and, after it was done, my impression of this person had increased. Because I had helped him, I actually liked him more.

The same thing happened when another friend called to tell me that he had recently been accepted to an MBA program. Since I had graduated from the same program three years prior, I agreed to help him develop his job-interviewing skills. The process of giving help was so positive that I wound up jumping through multiple hoops to get him an interview at my company. I did not have to do this, but he made me feel so helpful that I wanted to help even more.

I call this the "helping high." It's the feeling one gets while serving others—a feeling of gratification that spurs additional help and unselfishness. It's the feeling that you want to cultivate as you find mentors in your organization.

Finding mentors is a win-win situation. You, the mentee, get the help you need; they, the mentors, get the good feeling of helping someone out. Mentors can help you in a number of ways—ways that your boss may not be able to help you. There are four primary things that you want to look for in a mentor.

- Experience: Mentors should have more experience than you in a given field. Their expertise and advice should be very helpful to you.
- Title: If your mentor is in your organization, it is helpful, but not necessary, to have a mentor who has a title that carries some weight. She can be an advocate for you at higher levels, which pays off down the road.
- Unbiased: Make sure your mentor is someone who is willing to tell things to you straight. Structure the relationship so that there are no conflicts of interest. You should be in the "safe zone" when you speak to your mentor. While you can learn a lot from your boss, he is not your mentor.
- Connections: A mentor on your side is like a having a slam-dunk letter of recommendation with your name on it in your pocket at all times.

There is no limit to the number of mentors that you can have. Pick people from all walks of life who have different skills, experiences, and connections. I personally have several mentors. Each has something different to offer, be it connections or perspective or skills. The last two internal job opportunities that I have secured at my current company have been a direct result of a mentor helping me get there. Those few lunches that I scheduled with these mentors have already paid off several times over for me.

Getting people to agree to a mentor-mentee relationship can be easy. The key is to make it easy for them to say yes. This is accomplished by clearly laying out for them why you need a mentor, why he or she is the perfect mentor, and exactly how much time you are asking of them.

I prefer to write letters to potential mentors because it formalizes the request. A thoughtful letter typically elicits a thoughtful response. One of my current mentors is an executive with another company within my industry. Two years ago I wrote him a letter and asked if he'd be willing to be my mentor. Here is the request letter than I sent him:

> Mr. Dawson,
>
> Greetings! My name is Sam Owens. You and I spoke over the phone two years ago when I was nearing graduation from my MBA program. I was introduced to you by my father-in-law who thought it would be helpful for us to chat. Your advice two years ago was very valuable to me.
>
> I've thought about our conversation this past couple of years and wondered if you'd be willing to have more of them in the future. Simply put, the reason I'm writing you is to ask if you would be willing to be a mentor to me for the next couple of years, and perhaps beyond that. Your

career path is one that I admire and I believe that your mentorship would be invaluable to my professional development. Specifically, I'd like to meet with you a couple of times a year. For each meeting, I'd have a few marketing-related questions prepared to spark discussion, and may ask your advice on a current business challenge that I face at work. I may even ask you about current challenges you see facing the industry from your current position. I know you're busy, so I want to make this low key and take as little of your time as possible.

If you'd be willing to do this, let me suggest our first meeting while I'm in town visiting family this August. May I take you to lunch either Monday, August 1, or Tuesday, August 2? I will follow up with you in two weeks to see if you'd be willing to do this.

I look forward to hearing from you.

Best Regards,

Sam Owens

Chapter Summary

- To get things done at your company, you can choose to use either power or persuasion.

- Persuasion is a far more effective tool to use over the long term.

- The five principles of getting things done through persuasion are:

  a. Principles #1: Get your co-workers to genuinely like you by doing the following

     i.   Build a relationship before you need something

     ii. Perform random acts of kindness

     iii. Write handwritten notes to your co-workers

     iv. Send a complimentary note to their boss

     v.   Ask for help

     vi. Demonstrate loyalty

  b. Principles #2: Establish respect: It is important to be liked, but it's better to be respected.

  c. Principles #3: Be consistent.

  d. Principles #4: Ask for and follow up on commitments.

  e. Principles #5: Find mentors.

7

SKILL #6: MANAGING OTHERS–
BECOME A TALENT MAGNET

"HEY SAM, CAN YOU COME INTO MY OFFICE FOR A FEW MIN-utes for a quick chat?" It was my VP—the general manager of a business that grossed about $800 million in annual sales. This VP had experience, organizational power, and a personal bank account balance that was in a complete-ly different league from most employees, including myself. I worked on his business as an associate marketing manager and was about three years into my tenure at the company. I suppose I had earned his trust enough to where he was willing to confide in me on some work-related issues.

"I've just gotten my official employee engagement feedback from the team and I was really surprised by a few things." He then went on to tell me that the feedback he had gotten was not what he expected it to be. Employees on his team responded very negatively to questions like, *I feel like I have the authority to make decisions as it relates to my business*, and *I feel em-powered by leadership to do my job*. The results didn't make sense to him. The business was doing well, as was his career. Every time he interacted with his team they seemed to be really happy and upbeat. How could these survey results indicate that there was a problem and that some people weren't happy? This highly competent executive of a huge, growing business was getting feedback that he wasn't the boss he thought he was. He was completely floored.

Fast-forward five years and I'm sitting in a friend's office at another company. "My team hates me, Sam. I've recently gotten survey results back that say that my team doesn't feel valued. They don't think that they are involved in any critical decisions and feel like cogs in a machine. I've been working so hard to turn this business around. It stinks to hear that, after all my hard work, my team thinks I'm a bad manager."

In neither of these situations did I try to solve the problem. Rather, I chose to lend a listening ear and to be empathetic and supportive. But these and many other experiences throughout my career have taught me three lessons about managers: First, managers are like car drivers—the majority of them believe they are above average. Second, poor managers are shocked when they find out what their co-workers really think of them. Third, most poor managers are really good people, with really good intentions.

In every organization, there are people that no one wants to work for. I call these people "talent repellers," and everyone knows who they are. I've now worked for four different corporations in my career and, within the first two months at each company, I have discovered who the bad managers were. Employees love to talk—especially about their bosses—and it's been easy to find out who the good and bad eggs were. In both of the personal examples I provided above, I already knew what they were going to tell me before they spoke. Several employees had already told me what they were like to work for. Both of them were talent repellers, and while they were certainly great at most areas of their jobs, their management style held them back from reaching their potential.

On the other hand, there are people in organizations whom everyone wants to work for. These are the talent magnets. Like talent repellers, everyone knows who they are and fights to work for them. Talent magnets, like talent repellers, are smart (although they don't have to be the smartest) and competent employees. The way they manage people is fundamentally different from talent repellers. This is a strategic advantage for them in their career.

Does Being a Talent Magnet Matter?

I mentioned earlier in this book that your relationship with your manager is the most important relationship you have at work. That is true, but your second most important relationship is the relationship you have with those you manage. Having smart, talented, and motivated people under you affords you great leverage in your daily work. Consider the following benefits of having great talent working for you:

1. **Magnification:** Simple arithmetic shows that two people are better than one, three people are better than two, and so on. If you are willing to give up a little of your control to other people, you can amplify the impact you have at work without killing yourself in the process.

2. **Complementary Skills:** Most people are really good at only a few things. You want people with skills that round out your weaknesses. Employees with complementary skills to yours can keep you out of a lot of trouble at work.

3. **Reputation:** If you stand out as a good manager, word will travel fast. You will have people competing to be on your team. Not only that, but your reputation will follow you to other jobs. In the connected, "LinkedIn" world we live in today, it's not hard for people to find out your management style before they even start working for you.

4. **Career Progression:** Linked to reputation, your management skills will be either an asset or a liability as it relates to getting promoted. When leadership teams decide who to promote and who to leave in place, management style is an important consideration that gets more important the higher you get.

5. **Karma:** As you progress in your career, you may have someone who used to work for you be in a position to be your boss someday. At my last company, a vice-president of research and development was working for someone who he personally hired out of college several years prior. Good thing he was kind while he was in charge! Be careful how you treat people while you have the power.

Unfortunately, way too many bosses don't understand how critical it is to manage other people well—and if they do understand it, they don't behave as if they do. These are talented people who know how to get the work done and how to manage their bosses to make themselves look good. Yet they don't get the fact that they are fighting with one hand tied behind their backs and, if they would just learn how to manage their teams properly, they would unlock an entirely new dimension of capacity that would propel their careers even faster.

According to one study from the Gallup Organization[6], seventy percent of employee engagement is determined by direct managers. Now for the bad part of the equation: Only thirty percent of US workers report that they are engaged at work. Thus, when an employee's engagement rests primarily on the manager's shoulders, and only thirty percent of employees are engaged, it's obvious that managers have some work to do.

This is not human resources fluff. This is real dollars and cents. One study[7] estimated employee turnover rate in 2015 to be at sixteen percent per year, meaning that every year, one out of six people at your company will quit. It is further estimated that every time an employee quits, it costs the employer anywhere from sixteen to twenty percent of an employee's annual salary to hire and train a new employee, according to the Center for American Progress[8]. On a national level, this equates to billions of dollars wasted per year! If you don't believe it, just wait until you have an employee quit on you, and then track the number of hours you and your HR partner spend on finding someone new instead of doing your job.

---

6   Employee Engagement Survey, Gallup Organization

7   CompData Survey 2015 Employee Turnover Nationally

8   There are significant business costs to replacing employees," Center of American Progress, November 2012

These crushing business expenses could be dramatically reduced by improving employee engagement, which is largely up to managers to create. Yes, being a talent magnet matters: to you and your career, to your employee and her career, and to your company's bottom line.

People Managers vs. Individual Contributors

Going from an individual contributor to a manager of people may be the biggest transition you will make in your career. It requires a completely different set of skills than the skills that brought you to that point. It's a fundamentally different mindset on how work gets done. In fact, if you are currently managing other people and haven't materially changed the way you are working, you are likely not doing your job right. You're probably driving your employees crazy, too.

Consider some examples of contrast in mindset between an individual contributor and people manager

Individual Contributor: My individual work ethic is what drives my success. I'm simply willing to work longer and harder than others.

People Manager: Knowing how to optimally leverage my team's unique abilities is what drives success.

Individual Contributor: If I want something done right, I have to do it myself.

People Manager: knowing when to do something myself, and when to step back and let someone else do it, is the key to high performance.

Individual Contributor: I spend my time working, studying, and gaining expertise.

People Manager: I spend my time coaching, mentoring, and helping my team gain expertise.

Individual Contributor: I am in all the details—that's where the answers are.

People Manager: I know which details to be in, and leave the rest to my team.

How to Be a Talent Repeller (A.K.A. What NOT to do)

Over the years, I've heard the following statements from co-workers:

> My boss is always in the weeds. I feel like every decision I make is being scrutinized and I have to keep him up to date on every detail of my business. If I don't, I get on his "bad" list very quickly.
>
> My manager is brilliant, I'll give him that. But he doesn't listen to other people's ideas. He always assumes he's the smartest person in the room and people notice it. It would be good if he would occasionally listen to experts before barking off his own ideas on how to solve problems.
>
> My boss has no regard for my time. Anything that is urgent to him has to be urgent for me.
>
> I haven't had a career conversation with my manager in about a year. It would be nice if he would actually show an interest in my career goals instead of always just asking for things that he needs. It feels like we have a transactional relationship.
>
> I know absolutely nothing about my manager's personal life, and he never asks about my personal life. I wonder

if he even knows that I'm a single mom trying to raise two kids on my own.

I have to watch my back around my manager because I think he would throw me under the bus if it meant that he would look good. I know for a fact that he would take care of his own career first.

It would be nice if I could show off my work a little to my vice-president, but my manager shamelessly takes credit for my work every time we are in a meeting together. I can only imagine how much credit she takes when I am not around.

I don't think my manager knows how much work I'm doing. She just keeps piling it on without any regard for everything else she's asked me to do. She hasn't asked me once about my workload.

Sometimes it's painful to watch my manager interact with her people. It's just so obvious that all she cares about is her own reputation and nothing else. I would love to see her make a decision once without thinking about how it will impact the way she looks in front of others.

These statements are commonplace at work. Why? Why are so many people apparently bad managers? Well, some bad managers are bad because they really just don't care. They don't care about being a good manager, nor do they care about the people they manage. I've found, however, that these people are rare in the corporate world. Most of the time, managers have the best of intentions. They want to build strong relationships with those that work for them and excel at managing them. They recognize the powerful leverage they can have by working

with them. Furthermore, bad managers are often good employees. If they know how to manage their managers, their bosses
love them. They are competent and hard-working—that's why
they've been promoted to their positions. But when it comes to
managing others, they are seriously lacking.

Consider the following categories of bosses with poor people management skills. Have you ever worked for someone
like this?

The Woodpecker: Have you ever gone into your boss to
present an analysis or an idea, and before you are done showing him the first page of the presentation, your boss has asked
you ten questions—mostly by interrupting you—and made ten
recommendations about how to improve the wording on the
first page? If so, you've got yourself a first-class woodpecker for
a boss. The woodpecker throws question after question at you
in a frenetic, unstructured way. It's not uncommon for you to
set up an hour meeting to present a structured analysis to this
boss, and then have your presentation completely derailed by
questions within the first five minutes.

The Savior: This well-intentioned boss is the one who
feels he has to solve all your problems for you. For example, if
you are in a healthy debate with another co-worker in front of
this type of boss, he will immediately step in to resolve the con-
flict. Or, if you express to your boss some concerns you have at
work, he immediately gives suggestions about how to solve the
problem before truly listening. And to make matters worse, he
honestly believes he is being helpful by hovering over you and
correcting your every mistake. This robs you of experience you
need to grow and develop.

The Goal-Post Mover: To put it nicely, this boss has a "continuous improvement" mentality. He asks for something, and when you give him what he asks for, he immediately asks for something else without even acknowledging any sort of progress or closure on the work you have done. Rather than pausing to help his employee feel like he is making progress, he just moves the "goal-post" back a few more feet, while you frantically keep running. Eventually, the employee comes to expect her boss to never acknowledge completion or even progress, and he either burns out or learns to compartmentalize a less-than-ideal work situation.

The Data Fiend: This boss has an insatiable appetite for data. He wants to see that data sliced, diced, and tortured. To justify her obsession with data, this boss will proudly say that she is "intellectually curious." The problem is, she usually doesn't have a good reason to keep her employees digging into the data. If she does, she isn't good at explaining it. This leaves employees feeling likes cogs in a machine because they aren't seeing what part their work plays in the big picture. Her fiendish desire for data causes her to put people on the spot. Employees don't usually like answering random facts about their business or doing math in their heads without being able to prepare. To the boss, it's just talking about the business. To the employee, it's a grueling quiz where he feels like he's being constantly tested and graded.

The Pleaser: This boss doesn't want to offend or alienate anyone or anything. Thus, he is reluctant to make any decisions or drive clarity, and he often reverses his decisions. In other words, this boss has a really tough time saying "No" to anyone. This leaves employees feeling confused and inefficient.

The Aligner: This boss doesn't take action, even on the smallest of decisions, unless his boss signs off on it. He is insecure in his ability to make his own decisions and terrified at the consequences of something going wrong. Making sure his boss approves everything is the way he protects himself. This behavior diminishes his credibility and effectiveness. Eventually, people don't go to him for direction because they know it will ultimately come from someone else.

The Usurper: This boss thinks he is taking things off of your plate by not giving you important projects and excluding you from important meetings. He takes any critical analysis or work you have done and uses it in meetings with his boss. He may pay you a compliment or two while showing your work to other people, or he might completely take credit himself. Either way, you aren't getting the exposure and experience you need to progress in your career.

The Worried Parent: This manager is constantly worried and does a terrible job hiding it. She's not only worried about her own job but does enough worrying for her whole team. She does this by casting doubt on the work you are trying to do by asking, "Are you sure about this analysis? I mean, I wonder if you need to triple-check those facts," or by saying, "I think you really need to be buttoned up if you are going to make such a bold recommendation." It's not just what she says but the fact that everything she says has a worried tone to it that makes everyone on their team feel constantly uneasy. This is horribly stressful for the team. When the boss is stressed, everyone is stressed.

The Crisis Creator: This boss positions everything as a crisis that needs to be solved immediately. For him, the world is constantly in free-fall and in desperate need of fixing. Everything is a priority, which basically means there is no clarity or prioritization among the team. Every day, employees walk in and wonder when the boss will walk by and completely blow up their day. They dread having their boss stop by because they know their day will completely change.

The Idealist: This manager thinks of herself as an optimist, but her team thinks she's an all-talk manager who has no concept of reality. She lays out grand visions without practical application. Over time, when her idealistic visions don't become realities, her team stops trusting her.

The "Guilty Until Proven Innocent" Crusader: Rather than assume employees are inherently smart and capable, this manager assumes his employees are dumb and incompetent until proven otherwise. He gives his employees a brief trial period to prove themselves. If they prove to be worthy of his endorsement, he gives it. Otherwise, his good opinion is gone. He will not "stick his neck out" for anyone until they have proven themselves to him.

So the first step in becoming a talent magnet is to not be a talent repeller. You must stop any of the negative behavior that they practice. Don't do that stuff.

How to Be a Talent Magnet (A.K.A. What to Do)

While managing people can be challenging, it's actually quite simple. Basic human needs are universal and unchanging. Managing others is not about keeping up with cutting-edge management techniques. Rather, it's about understanding the fundamentals of human needs and then developing the skills to appropriately nurture them. You can become a talent magnet with a little self-awareness and concerted effort.

Talent magnets have four critical attributes: They put people first, drive clarity among their teams, and customize their style to the individual, and they have high expectations of their people.

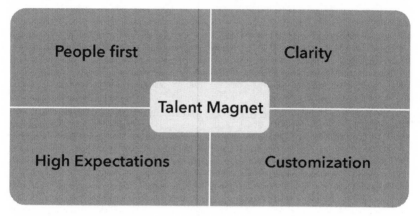

PEOPLE FIRST

I believe that an employee's most important need—and, believe me, employees have a lot of needs—is the need to feel valued. Feeling valued affects everything they do at work. When employees do not feel valued, they are more stressed, angry, and negative. Even if they are working hard and appear to be productive, employees that don't feel valued will not stick around very long. Over time, undervalued employees will learn to do what is asked of them and nothing more. On the other hand, employees who feel valued are motivated to go above and beyond what is asked of them. They are more resilient and optimistic, and are more likely to stay in their companies.

Talent magnets recognize that people are the most important component of a business and prioritize their actions accordingly. They deeply value their employees and, just as important, they are good at expressing it. They recognize that being valued is about more than just the money. A truly valued employee is valued both personally and professionally. This means that you, as a manager, have to find a way to connect personally with your employee on a level far more fundamental then what both of your job descriptions would indicate. What's more, you need to make them feel valued as a professional, to help them feel that the contribution they are making has an impact.

Below are some ways that you, as a talent magnet, can help your employees feel valued as people and professionals:

1. **Get to know them personally:** Take time to understand their particular situation in life and what their life goals are. To the degree they want you to, find out about their family, about their background, and about what passions or hobbies they have outside of work.

2. **Respect their time:** Managers are notorious for behavior that would indicate that they couldn't care less about their employee's time—always pulling them into last-minute meetings, showing up late or blowing off critical meetings, and keeping their employees over-allocated with meeting times. As a manager, you should respect your employees' time just like you want your time respected.

3. **Respect their private lives:** When they need to take care of a personal matter, accommodate it, even if it requires temporary inconvenience and sacrifice.

4. **Express genuine appreciation:** Don't just give the obligatory "thank you" or "you're the greatest," but find ways to show real appreciation for the unique contributions they make.

5. **Bring up their career progression more than they do:** A manager's natural inclination is to think more about their own career progression and less about their employee's career progression. Yet talent magnets recognize that their job as managers is to get their employees promoted. Part of helping employees feel valued is letting them know that you are thinking about what's next for them. You should be formally talking about this with your employee at least once per quarter. Informal conversations can happen more frequently. Ideally, you have set career goals together and review them periodically to track progress.

6. **Be an advocate for them to your boss:** There are many little things that can drive positive momentum with your employee: a simple positive email to your boss or public praise of your employee in a meeting. You can also schedule time with your boss and your employee to talk about your employee's career. This helps your boss feel invested in your employee, like you are. This effort will go a long way with those who work for you—they will never forget this.

CLARITY

Before entering corporate America, I believed that *likeability* was the key to great leadership. All I had to do to be a great leader, I thought, was to get others to like me. I believed this until I entered the workforce and heard others complain about their bosses. The complaints always seemed to start with, "My boss is a great person, but...", or "I really like the guy, but..." and then ended with harsh criticism. It turns out, I have learned, that likeability is a nice thing to have in a manager, but it's not essential. Clarity, on the other hand, is an *indispensable* quality in a good manager.

Clarity is the virtue that allows an employee to understand what success looks like and how to deliver against it. Clarity sets a target for an employee and gives them the tools to hit it. With clarity, employees feel like they are moving forward. Without it, they feel like they are running on a hamster wheel.

Being clear is different from being prescriptive. Many managers believe that they are being clear when they are really just micromanaging. This has the opposite effect of clarity. Being clear motivates employees; micromanaging drains them.

Here are some questions that can help you understand where you fall on the micromanager spectrum. Do you:

- Overly obsess about the formatting and specific words in your employee's PowerPoint presentations?
- Believe that no employee can do a job quite like you?
- Ask your employees to revise their work multiple times until the job is done *exactly* how you want it?
- Finish the work that your employees send to you so that you can change the wording and formatting to exactly how you want it?
- Try to exert control over not only what tasks are being done by your team, but *how* they are done?

- Make comments like, "I know this is a nit-picky thing" before making a really nit-picky and non-essential critique of your employee's work?
- Justify your behavior by saying to yourself and others that you are just trying to be efficient?

On the other hand, there are a lot of ways that managers can be clear without micromanaging. Here they are:

1. **Give them projects with ownership:** Assign projects for which they can have full accountability. How much free rein should you give them? Enough that, when challenges arise, you feel comfortable telling them, "This is your call, I'll support whatever decision you make." If the project is too big and risky to do that, then carve off a smaller chunk of a project for them so they own the decisions.

2. **Speak in terms of solving problems, not completing tasks:** Present an assignment as a problem to be solved, rather than a task to be completed, you are essentially saying, "You are a smart person, and I have confidence that you will figure this out."

3. **Set up clear deliverables:** Explain to them what you would like to see at the end of the project, and give them some intermediate things to deliver to track progress. This does not mean you tell them exactly how to get there or critique their unique thinking process (this would be micromanaging) but it does mean that you are clear about what success looks like.

4. **Provide your point of view:** Give them an example of how you think about the project and even how you would approach solving the problem. Many employees appreciate this guidance. However, always caveat that it is your approach and that other approaches can work, too, as long as the end project is strong.

How to give tough feedback to employees

Giving timely and accurate feedback to your employees is a critical component of clarity. A deadly sin committed by managers—especially new ones—is "feedback avoidance," or the unwillingness of managers to provide their employees with candid feedback. For whatever reason—discomfort with confrontation, lack of time, or poor communication skills—these managers don't prioritize clear feedback discussions with their employees. As a result, their employees aren't given the opportunity to improve. Too many employees spend weeks, months, years, and even entire careers working below their potential, in part because their managers were too afraid or too selfish to provide them with honest feedback about their performance and their standing within their organization.

Providing candid feedback to employees is good for the employee, boss, and company. It creates transparency and increases productivity. It enhances the employee-boss relationship by fostering a spirit of candor and trust. But it does require some know-how and shouldn't be taken lightly. While open feedback discussions are critical to continuous improvement, feedback delivered the wrong way can have disastrous consequences.

Here are a few guidelines to make sure that, when you feel it's time to have a feedback conversation, you get it right.

1. **Be timely:** When you've identified an opportunity for improvement, don't wait more than a day or two to give feedback. There are few things more demoralizing to an employee than hearing that the boss has had an issue with his performance for quite some time but chose not to tell him until the official performance review. Giving feedback immediately gives him a chance to fix the issue before the formal review and get back on track. Employees should never be surprised in a formal performance review because their bosses should be providing timely feedback all along the way.

2. **Prime the pump:** It's important not to catch your employee off guard. Before having the actual discussion with them, ask your employee either via email or in person to meet at a certain time to have a conversation. When you do this, make sure you let them know that you have some feedback for them and that that is what you want to talk about. This will give the employee time to mentally prepare for the conversation.

3. **Don't sugarcoat:** Don't tap dance around the feedback by using euphemisms and abstract words. Rather, use clear and simple language. You don't want the employee walking out of the meeting misunderstanding your message. This applies to both positive and negative feedback. If your employee does something extremely well, tell him. If he needs to improve in an area, tell him.

4. **Be specific:** Specific examples are the best way to illustrate your feedback because they are irrefutable. Saying that your employee is annoying is a highly debatable piece of feedback but saying that when your employee interrupted you five times in the last meeting that you found it distracting presents two irrefutable facts. First, he interrupted you five times. Second, you found it distracting.

5. **Listen:** All employees want to be heard and feel understood. Give your employee an opportunity to respond to your feedback. You may even be surprised to find that there is more to the story than you originally thought and this could potentially change your mind. Yet, even if it doesn't, your employee should at least feel that you listened.

6. **Infuse hope and optimism:** Remember that the purpose of giving feedback is to create opportunity for improvement. After you have provided the feedback to the employee, make sure you instill in him some hope. One way to do this would be to provide specific suggestions of how to improve and offer to coach them. Assure him that you have confidence that he will improve and get to where he wants to go in his career.

7. **Open yourself up to feedback:** To have relationships based on trust, feedback must go both ways. Employees should be allowed to give the boss feedback, so make sure to ask for feedback and give your employee an opportunity to be honest with you. If needed, let them have a couple of days to formulate their feedback and come back to you with it.

8. **Document the conversation:** It's just good re-cord-keeping to document any feedback conversations that you have with your employees, especially in very difficult situations where an employee may ultimately be terminated.

One size fits one

My wife Gina and I are constantly amazed by the stark difference in our children's personalities. They are being raised in the same environment. They have the same diet, the same rules, the same socioeconomic status, and the same religious and moral training. Yet their individual personalities are very different. They respond differently to discipline and leadership. They fundamentally value different things. For example, Mollie values community; she wants me to complete most tasks together with her. Charlotte, on the other hand, values independence; she wants to do everything herself without any help from me. Max values logic and reason; everything has to make logical sense to him. Getting our children to respond to us requires very different tactics based on what they value.

Employees have fundamentally different values, too. Sure, they all are at work because they need to make a living and they all generally want to be treated with respect. Money and respect in the workplace are basic necessities in order for employees to survive. But surviving is different from thriving and, if you really get to know your employees, you'll discover the one or two things that make them *thrive*. It is not the same for everyone. For example, I've worked with someone who valued recognition above all else. He was a creative artist and, while he needed money to survive, recognition and appreciation for his work truly invigorated him. Another employee solely cared about achievement and efficiency. As long as she felt like she was getting things done in an efficient manner, she was happy. Another employee just wanted to get promoted. For her, it wasn't about the money. It was about the feeling that she was moving up in the world and making progress in her life.

Here are some examples of things that your employees could value above all else:

- Individual respect
- Autonomy
- Ownership
- Rewards
- Recognition (either one-on-one or in front of large groups)
- Money, money, and more money
- Title and prestige
- Work-life balance
- Learning and development
- The thrill of accomplishment
- A challenging work environment
- A belief in an idea or vision
- Safety and harmony
- Contribution
- Sense of community
- Intellectually stimulating work

So take note: If you have insight into what matters to your employees, you will be that much more effective as a manager. You can give them projects that cater to their deepest values.

HIGH EXPECTATIONS

In college, I noticed a trend that I call the teacher-student paradox. Students, including myself, at the beginning of the semester were always thrilled to hear when the professor of a new class was easy. It meant that there would be little to no homework, the academic concepts would be easy to grasp, and most of us would get a good grade. Yet slowly, as the semester progressed, something changed. We started to lose interest in the class and lose respect for the teacher. Because the class was so easy, we didn't feel like we were learning anything. We were bored out of our minds, and we had no sense of challenge or accomplishment. By the end of the semester, we were feeling less thrilled about our good grade and more disappointed that we had wasted our time. Sure, we could have taken the initiative ourselves and gone above and beyond what was expected of us, but what college student does that?

I've mentioned earlier in this chapter that valuing your employees is a critical component of being a talent magnet. Feeling challenged is the other. A great manager must understand the balance between these two and not let one consistently override the other. For example, if a manager spends all his time challenging his employee without making him feel valued, then the employee will burn out. On the other hand, if an employee is always valued but never challenged, the employee will be bored.

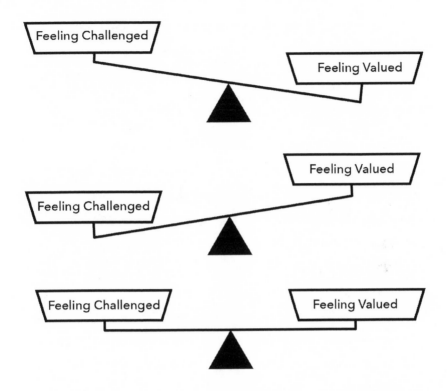

Challenging an employee is not just about stretching their capabilities; it's about making them proud to do the work that they do. You can do this by establishing a culture of excellence on your team. Here are the main principles behind doing this.

- First, it all starts with you. The work that you do needs to be excellent work that sets an example for your team. Show them through your work what excellent looks like.
- Second, you need to be the steward of your team's priorities. Everyone wants to be excellent. But requiring your team to be excellent at everything is called slave-driving. This is not challenging your employees. Rather, it's being an unreasonable boss whom em-

ployees resent. As a manager, you decide which two or three things your team must be excellent at in order to be successful. You should be relentless with those things, and lenient about the other things. On my marketing team, for example, I expect my team to be excellent at all activities related to generating consumer demand for our products. That means that our advertising must be impeccable. It means that our sales presentations are flawless and clear. It also means that for most other things, like managing budgets and crunching numbers, eighty percent of the way there is generally good enough.

- Third, you must know your employee's limits. A nice challenge to one employee might be easy to another, yet completely overwhelming to another.

Chapter Summary

- The relationship you have with your direct reports is the second most important relationship you have at work.

- Becoming a talent magnet—someone that people want to work for—can be a huge advantage to you with the following benefits:
  - Magnification of your influence and impact at work
  - Added skills that complement your own
  - Increased reputation at your company
  - Better career progression
  - Good Karma!

- Going from individual contributor to people manager requires two completely different mindsets.

- Talent repellers come in many forms, including:
  - The Savior
  - The Goal-Post Mover
  - The Data Fiend
  - The Pleaser
  - The Aligner
  - The Usurper
  - The Worried Parent
  - The Crisis Creator
  - The Idealist
  - The "Guilty Until Proven Innocent" Crusader

- Talent magnets focus on doing four things
  1. People first
     a. Get to know them personally.

    b. Respect their time.

    c. Respect their private lives.

    d. Express genuine appreciation.

    e. Bring up their career progression more than they do.

    f. Be an advocate for them to your boss.

7. Clarity

    a. Give them projects with ownership.

    b. Speak in terms of solving problems, not completing tasks.

    c. Set up clear deliverables.

    d. Provide your point of view.

5. Customization

    a. Recognize that your employees value different things. Tailor your assignments and style to what they care about and you'll get more out of them.

2. High expectations

    a. Carefully balance the "feeling valued" and "feeling challenged" equation.

8

SKILL #7: EVOLVING–
STAY MARKETABLE

IMAGINE FOR A MOMENT THAT YOU WERE BORN IN 1920. You grew up in a middle-class family, graduated from high school, and then were drafted into the Army to fight in World War ll. After the war, you had the good fortune of going to college and obtaining a college degree before entering the workforce. Upon graduation, you took a desk job at a reputable company. The job provided a steady paycheck and stability. You got married, bought a house, and had a family. Over the next few years the company treated you well and you got a few promotions. At this point, you started to make some decent money. A few more years go by and you had an opportunity to go into business with a couple of friends. After careful consideration, you eventually decided to decline the offer. After all, you enjoyed your paycheck and your pension was getting more and more valuable every day. Furthermore, it was the 60's and you had your hands full with teenagers who were talking about free love and listening to a lot of Janice Joplin. Starting a new business would have put way too much stress on your family, so you opted to stick it out at your company. A couple more decades went by, your kids have left the house, and you were ready to retire. By that point, you had spent forty years with the same company. On the last day of your retirement, the company threw you a going-away party, complete with a gold-plated watch as a send-off gift. And, most importantly, you had earned yourself a fully vested pension that will take care of you the rest of your life.

Those were the good old days. Today's business climate, however, is dramatically different from what I just described. Unlike the post-World War ll economy, where there seemed to be an unwritten agreement of "You stick it out with the company and we'll take care of you," today's economy is much more focused on employees taking care of themselves. Just one example of this change is the way companies think about retirement for their employees. Defined benefits plans, most commonly known as pensions, are nearly extinct. Instead, companies have migrated to "defined *contribution* plans," the most popular being the 401(K) plan. Defined benefits plans basically represented a promise that an employer would provide a monthly income stream to an employee upon retirement, based on the number of years worked at the company, salary level, and other factors. Defined contribution plans, on the other hand, are designed such that the employer matches a contribution first made by the employee.

According to a 2010 US Treasury report on retirement plans,[9] the percentage of active participants in employer-spon

---

9 *Statistical Trends in Retirement Plans*, US Treasury, 2010

sored pensions went from 65.8% to 22.5% from 1977 to 2007. Over the same time period, the number of participants in employer-sponsored defined contribution plans went from 34.2% to 77.5%.

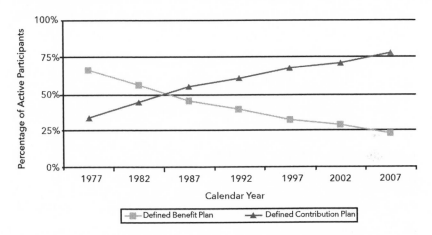

This trend sends a clear and sobering message to employees today: You—not your company—are responsible for your retirement.

Retirement planning is just one factor contributing to the decreased loyalty between corporations and employees. I believe many other factors—advances in technology, globalization, economic progress of emerging markets, and a good fifty-plus year run of relative U.S. peace and prosperity—have driven this trend. Regardless of the drivers and whether or not you believe this reality is good or bad, the facts proving that loyalty is declining are irrefutable. US workers today change employers, on average, every 4.2 years[10]. Project that out over a 30-year career and you will likely change jobs over 8 times in your career!

---

10 Bureau of Labor Statistics Employee Tenure Summary, released September 22, 2016

Succeeding in today's disloyal corporate culture will require you to operate differently from your grandparents. You will need to employ two strategies during your career. The first one, which is the strategy your grandparents used, is that of performing well and, thus, moving up the ladder at your current company. The second strategy, which your grandparents did not have to play, is that of always assessing your external options and being ready to make a job switch when you need to. The first strategy is essentially the subject of this book. The second is what I'll discuss in detail in this chapter.

When Is It Time to Leave Your Company?

Why would you leave a perfectly stable job? There are several reasons why you might decide that it's time to leave, including:

Misery: You can't stand your boss, the people you work with, your hours, the day-to-day work, or all of the above. Perhaps you have been moved to a different department with a different culture. Perhaps your interests have changed and what used to stimulate you professionally doesn't do it for you anymore. Whatever the reason, you no longer enjoy your job and you've got to get out.

Career runway: You have gotten signals that you are not on the "fast track" for promotion. You realize that your upside for making more money will either take longer than you think it should or that you won't ever get another promotion at the company. When pushing for a promotion with your boss, you get sick of hearing the run-around responses like, "I think you just need more time in your role," or "I think we need to see x, y, and z before you can get to the next level." Granted, these things aren't necessarily bad things to hear...the first or second time. But when it becomes a multi-year pattern, your company is sending you a signal.

Competitive comparison: You see friends that you graduated with getting promoted—friends that you know you can compete with. You are hearing about jobs that make more money that you are highly qualified for. If you determine that you can make more money or have more career longevity—or both—somewhere else, it's a great time to look for a new job.

Opportunity: You find an opportunity that you can't refuse—a cause that you are particularly passionate about or a compensation package that would be crazy to turn down.

Life stage: At some point during your career, priorities change. Life becomes less about you and more about your loved ones. This will affect the career choices you make. For example, you may be next in line for a nice career promotion with your company but the promotion requires you to move across the country. Since you have kids in high school, you decide that staying in one place is more important than getting a VP job. So, you look around locally and find a job that pays less and doesn't have as much upside but allows you to stay in one spot.

Regardless of *why* you leave, the fact is that at some point you likely *will* leave, and therefore will need to keep your job-landing skills current. These skills will be relevant and important to you throughout your career, all the way up until you retire. These skills can get you a pay raise at a different job that is a better fit for your unique abilities. If you are ever let go in a mass layoff, job-landing skills can help you secure a job quickly so you are not unemployed for an extended period of time. They will be skills that you will use over and over.

You may not be currently looking for a job. In this case, my hope is that this chapter will serve as a reference for you in the future. If you believe the job-switching statistics that I shared earlier, you will be job hunting again within the next one to four years. On the other hand, if you *are* currently looking for a job, this chapter gives you the skills you need to beat your competition and get the job you want.

The Job-Landing Process

In college, job hunting is taught as though it were a math problem. According to the people at your typical college career center, the process seems fairly simple and objective. The pathway, it seems, is a four-step process:

1. You apply for a job that matches your skills.
2. Your potential employer interviews you.
3. You receive a job offer.
4. You accept the job offer and live happily ever after.

This formulaic process sounds almost like an arranged marriage, in which two parties are paired together in an objective, transactional way. There is little emotion involved. If everything looks good on paper, then the transaction is made

If only it were that easy! In reality, finding a job is much less like an arranged marriage and much more like dating, where two consenting individuals come together to explore an opportunity with the ultimate goal of falling in love with each other. Unlike arranged marriages, courtships can be highly emotional, subjective, and uncertain. There can be ups and downs in the courting process, with no guarantees that it will work out. Each party may come to the table with a little "baggage," and may be "seeing" other people without telling one another. The whole ordeal can get very dramatic!

The job search is a highly imperfect process. There are many variables in play, some of which are out of your control. Yet, while you can't control everything, there are indeed some tried and true job-landing practices that will make sure that you come out on top more often than not.

The job-landing process can be broken into two phases, and this chapter will focus on one at a time:

Phase 1: Getting the Interview: Once you have found a company that interests you, your primary goal should be to secure a job interview with that company. This includes getting on the company's radar through networking, informational interviewing, and creating a fantastic resume.

Phase 2: Nailing the Interview: After you have secured an interview, your focus shifts to ensuring that you are completely prepared to succeed in the interview. You must over-prepare in order to beat the competition that you will undoubtedly have. In my last job interview, I prepared for over twenty hours. After getting the job, I found out that I was competing against over ten other interviewees for the same job. I likely could have spent two hours preparing and done fine. But fine would not have gotten me the job.

Part 1: Getting the Interview

A corporation may have thousands of resumes floating around in its database. Some of these resumes have been glanced at by recruiters and brushed to the side because they are difficult to read or have glaring spelling errors. Other resumes are quickly skimmed from top to bottom and then disqualified because they don't meet a key pre-requisite stated in the job description, such as a college degree or a certain number of years of experience in an industry. Still others just don't read in a clear and concise manner. A moderately experienced recruiter will know how to screen these resumes out as well. These resumes are the easy ones. Recruiters can sniff them out and throw them in the trash without working that hard.

But then there are the "hard" resumes. These resumes are well-written, show relevant experience, and meet the requirements of the job description. Such resumes are very difficult for recruiters to deal with. There may still be tens—even hundreds—of quality resumes to look at, even after all the bad ones are filtered out. Clearly, there isn't enough time or resources for the company interview each candidate. In fact, there is barely time for the recruiter to *read* each resume.

It is this conundrum that has always fascinated and haunted me, as I've wondered how recruiters handle this dilemma. How do they think about resumes? Which resumes get picked and why? What separates a *great* resume from a sea of *good* ones? These questions have caused me to agonize over my own resume, meticulously revising and re-thinking its formatting, wording, and tone. In school, I spent countless hours making sure that my resume was in the best possible shape. Yet, now that I have experience on the other side—that is, with screening resumes and picking candidates myself—I see the fatal flaw in my fastidious resume-revising approach. I've learned that, on paper, the resume is the number one tool in evaluating a candidate but, in practice, the resume is just the entry point. There are many other tools that you can use to gain an advantage.

Before going any further, let's define the key players in the hiring process and lay out how much power is wielded by each:

Recruiter: The recruiter generally works in the human resources department, supporting one or more business units. Recruiters do most of the leg work in finding people to interview, including screening resumes and making introductory calls. But the recruiter almost never makes the final hiring decision. That decision is made by the hiring manager.

The recruiter's primary motive is to keep the hiring manager happy by providing him with a narrowed-down list of strong candidates to interview. If the recruiter brings an impressive list of individuals to the hiring manager, then it's a job well done. If the list is weak, then it's a fail. Depending on the company and the position, there can be a fair amount of pressure on the recruiter and he is looking to make sure that the candidate list is as strong as possible. You should care about the recruiter because he has influence over the initial list. He is the gatekeeper. Without the recruiter, you will never make it past the first step.

Hiring manager: The hiring manager is your future boss. He will ultimately make the final decision regarding your employment. He isn't motivated by making other people happy. Rather, he has an open position to fill and wants someone good to fill it. In this sense, he has the most at stake because he has to live with his final decision—good or bad—for the foreseeable future. He recognizes that nothing can make a job easier than having a great employee under you and that nothing can make the job more exhausting and frustrating than an employee who isn't qualified.

Hiring manager peers: These are individuals who work with the hiring manager and are at his same career level. For example, if the hiring manager is a director, then his peers are other directors. They are important because there is a good chance they will interview you as well and the hiring manager will rely heavily on their assessment of you. He will ask them the classic hiring manager question: "Would you want this person on your team?"

Future peers: These are individuals who will be at your same career level should you be given the job. If you are invited to interview with the company, these individuals may show you around or take you to lunch. Their objective is to be informal friends of whom you can ask questions and resolve concerns about the job. While they do not wield a ton of influence, they could be asked to evaluate you nonetheless, so do not let your guard down completely while you are with them!

Now that we have those definitions clear, let's go back to the fundamental problem that a recruiter faces—that of too many good resumes and too little time. What is he to do? Or, even better, what are *you* to do in order to stand out? Remember the recruiter's motives—to keep the hiring manager happy with a strong pipeline of candidates. But with such little time, there is a lot of pressure and a lot of risk on the recruiter. So your job is to reduce that pressure by making it easy for him to say yes to you, and the first way to do this is through a stellar resume.

The four "R's" of a great resume

I have been involved with corporate recruiting for eight years now. I've mostly hired highly ambitious MBA students who want marketing jobs. I have personally witnessed how employees at all levels evaluate resumes and make decisions based on those evaluations. Basically, people judge resumes based on four key criteria—the "four Rs." They are readability, relevance, responsibility, and results.

Readability: This criterion is more of a necessity than a true differentiator. If your resume is difficult to follow, has spelling or grammatical errors, or is over one page in length, it is likely to get trashed. Thus, you need to make sure your resumes can be read easily. Here are the basic fundamentals to make sure your resume passes the readability test:

1. **It is placed in a common format that is easy to follow.** There are multiple resume templates out there. The simpler the better. You don't get extra points for having a flashy format but you can get your resume trashed if it is too distracting. So, avoid special colors and fancy formats. Run an online search on "MBA resumes templates," and you will find a wealth of them to choose from.

2. **It is the appropriate length.** Keep it to one page unless you have well over five years of full-time, post-college work experience. Even with over five years of experience, don't belabor your resume. Be concise.

3. **It is free of spelling mistakes and typos.** This is a very easy way for corporations to weed out people who aren't serious enough to proofread their resume.

4. **It is ordered chronologically, with easy-to-follow dates**. Potential employers want to see the timing of how you went from one experience to the next. They will also look for time-lapses in your resume where you were unemployed or doing something else and they will seek to reconcile the reason for the gaps. If you have big gaps of unemployment, you'll likely need to explain yourself in the interview.

5. **It uses action statements:** Resumes have a particular verbiage that is used. Each bullet point starts with an action statement like "Led," or "Managed," or "Contributed to," or "Developed."

6. **It leaves out superfluous words:** Write your sentences as a robot would write a sentence. Only the most important words should be included. For example, "I led a team of twenty-five people to program a video game. Then, we sold the game to different companies and made $100,000 a year," should read like this: "Led team of twenty-five professionals to program a video game, generating $100,000 in annual revenue."

Relevance: Assuming your resume meets the readability requirement, recruiters will quickly scan it to see if your experience is a fit for the job. They do this by looking for the companies you have worked for and your function within the company. For example, if you are applying for a position as a financial analyst at Wal-Mart, it will be to your advantage if you currently work as a financial analyst at Target.

Unfortunately, many people do not have the luxury of having their experience perfectly match the job description. In these circumstances, you will need to do some translation work. I call this "bridging." With this technique, you are building a figurative bridge between your experience and the required experience listed in the job description. For example, suppose you are applying for an entry-level job as a financial analyst at IBM Corporation but all your experience has been in sales. The job description states that you need to demonstrate proficient financial analytical skills. You don't feel like you have the background to demonstrate it.

This is where your creativity comes into play—find a way to demonstrate your skills. Perhaps you led projects in school that required you to analyze budgets or lead a project that was data-heavy. Or maybe your sales job required you to analyze the size and scope of your customer base.

Another example would be if the job description listed "excellent verbal and written communication skills." While you may not have experience as a professional journalist or public speaker, you certainly can find examples in your academic or professional life where you have communicated effectively to get something done.

Responsibility: Recruiters like to get a feel for the scope of work that you did. In other words, think of your mother, or little brother, or sixteen-year-old cousin. If they were to read your resume, would they understand your experience, or would they be completely confused? Was the budget you managed $500,000 or $50,000,000? Do you currently manage a team of people or are you an individual contributor? Are you in charge of the creative design of the print advertisement or are you an order taker? Most recruiters aren't readily familiar with your old company and position, so you have to break it down for them in very simple terms.

These questions can be quickly answered through a *responsibility statement*. This is a one- or two-sentence statement included with each job that you've had that describes exactly what you did. It should be placed directly below your job title and directly above your bulleted results statements.

Responsibility Statement

> **The Awesome Consumer Goods company, New York, NY**
> *Senior Brand Manager*
> *Managed $200MM cleaning products business. Led all aspects of marketing mix including pricing, advertising, consumer promotions, product innovation, and packaging design*
> • *Results statement 1*
> • *Results statement 2*
> • *Results statement 3*

The responsibility statement is meant to help the recruiter quickly grasp what you did in a particular role. It is not a "showoff" statement. It is simply meant to give the recruiter understanding. Provide just the facts of what you have done in the responsibility statement, and then you can show off later.

Results: With the first three "Rs" completed, your resume now looks like eighty percent of good resumes out there. The recruiter has now scanned your resume and understands that you can write coherently, that you know how to use spell check, that you have relevant experience, and that you have had decent responsibilities in your job. This is where the recruiter says to himself "good—so what?"

That's where results come in. Showing results takes your resume from average to excellent. Results show the recruiter that you have achieved success at your current and prior employers and are thus likely to achieve it in the future. Without showing results on your resume, it will be difficult for a recruiter to give your resume the approval stamp—even if you have all the other elements.

I learned this the hard way as I was looking for full-time jobs out of my MBA program. I was interested in working for a top-notch consumer goods firm. I had a great contact within the company and he liked me. As a courtesy, he reviewed my resume and said, in his own words, that it had met the first three Rs. He then said that I should re-word some of my bullet points to show more results. I didn't think his advice was critical, so I submitted my resume to the company without making the change. After all, I was busy and had satisfied the first three Rs. And, since I was confident that I would get the interview anyway, I didn't change anything.

Two months later, it was time to submit resumes for the position. To my great disappointment, I was not selected for an interview. When I went to career services and asked if the company had any feedback for me, the recruiting director replied, "They felt like your resume didn't have enough results." Ouch.

Even when you know people within the company and your resume has the right experience, you cannot expect to be selected for an interview unless you can prove that you've done something valuable in your prior experience.

Good results statements start with strong verbs and end in specific quantifiable outcomes. The magic is in the wording. You are not being deceptive here—you are telling the truth well.

Feeling bashful? Don't. This is not the time for modesty; it's the time for you to brag about your talents. And don't worry about not having meaty experience. Even if you are coming out of college and have only worked part-time jobs, there is always a way to demonstrate that you are results-driven.

The key to results statements is that they are specific and quantifiable. Anyone can put in a resume that says they are a leader or a self-starter, but not so many can give specific examples of those attributes. Let's suppose you managed a bowling alley for a year. Chances are that if you think about it enough, you can find a way to quantify some results that you achieved. Here are some examples:

- Grew sales by 20% by executing "buy one, get one" offer on Tuesday evenings to drive incremental customer visits (translation: nobody was coming in on Tuesdays, so I started giving people better deals).

- Cut costs by 18% over 6 months by revising employee schedules and changing suppliers (translation: I told employees that they couldn't work overtime anymore and I told one of our food suppliers to give us a better deal or we'd find someone else).

- Led analysis of food court menu to introduce new items and drive food sales growth of 8% (translation: Who in the world doesn't offer pizza at a bowling alley? Well, we didn't, and I thought we should. It worked pretty well when we started offering it).

- Reduced employee turnover by three people a year (25%) via implementing employee training programs and flexible work schedule (translation: People hated the old manager, and thought I was pretty reasonable, so more of them stuck around).

Whether you are an investment banker or waiter or custodian, there is always a way to quantify what you've done, and demonstrate that you are someone who can get results.

INFORMATIONAL INTERVIEWING

Imagine you are sitting at your work desk in the late afternoon, thinking about where you want to go for dinner this Friday. You go online to research available restaurants and you are inundated with a list of hundreds of places to choose from. You don't want to sort through the entire list, so you create parameters for your search. You want something with great reviews, affordability, and service. So, you eliminate those restaurants with terrible service reviews, as well as the ones with too many dollar signs next to them. With these parameters, you still have a sizeable list. Then you decide you want either Italian or Mexican food. You eliminate all other cuisine types. Even with these parameters, there are still around twenty-five Mexican or Italian Restaurants that have good reviews. At this point, you are getting hungry and frustrated.

Suddenly, a trusted friend walks past you to say hello. Noticing the list of restaurants on the screen, he sees "Abuelo's Casa," on your list. "I love Abuelo's Casa! I was there last week and it was delicious," he says. "Their tacos are great, the waiter I had was really helpful, and I thought the prices were super reasonable – especially for the portions."

Done! You close your computer and start to make your way out of your apartment en route to Abuelo's Casa. Your search is over.

Recruiters face situations like this all the time—not necessarily with restaurant decisions, but with selecting candidates for job interviews. When a recruiter is sitting on a stack of great resumes—those that have all 4 R's—and is running out of time, he is grateful for a personal reference from a co-worker. In fact, a personal reference from someone else in the company is almost a guarantee that a candidate's resume will get pulled from the pile, provided the resume is good. This is why corporations will often pay referral bonuses to employees. Companies know that one of the best ways to recruit is through its own employees.

In my experience, candidates who have personal recommendations from an employee get pulled out into the short list. It is a sure-fire way to make it easy for the recruiter to say "Yes" to you as a candidate. Knowing this, your first tactic in landing a job interview should be to establish a personal contact with people within your company of interest.

The keyword I'd like to emphasize is *"personal."* In order for an employee to feel comfortable enough to recommend you, the connection needs to be more than an invitation to connect on LinkedIn or an email asking for help. There needs to be two-way communication. The employee must feel a personal connection of some sort with you in order to recommend you to co-workers.

The most productive way to forge a connection is through informational interviewing—a thirty- to sixty-minute phone call or in-person meeting with someone who works for a company that interests you. The informational interview accomplishes two critical objectives. First, it gives you an opportunity to learn about the company. This can help you gain an advantage should you be invited to interview. You can learn much more about how a company really works by a thirty-minute conversation with an actual employee than you can by reading the recruiting section of the company's website or annual report. Second, it provides a chance for the employee to get to know you such that he or she would be comfortable recommending you. This is your chance to impress.

The beauty of the informational interview is its pleasant, low-pressure nature. Unlike a traditional, high-stakes job interview where the hiring manager asks pre-determined questions and rigorously evaluates you, informational interviews are more friendly and casual in nature. The conversation is largely in your control.

I have asked several people over the years for an informational interview. In each case, it has been a highly rewarding experience. In the best cases, interviews such as these have gotten me a job interview. In the worst cases, they have allowed me to make another valuable business contact and learn something new. I've never had one person turn me down for this kind of interview and I've never had a single negative interview experience. People are happy to perform a favor and even more happy to talk about themselves.

There are many ways to find people who work for your company of interest. LinkedIn is a fantastic database where you can find nearly anyone you want, at any level in an organization, at any company. Using your school's alumni network is another excellent tool. Few things tug on the heartstrings more than the ol' alma mater. Besides these tools, you can use church, neighborhood, social media, and civic contacts. If you have your antennae tuned in, you will find what you are looking for.

Let's look at an example of a great informational interview:

EXAMPLE

Mike is a student interested in working in the e-commerce industry and he has a specific interest in being a retail buyer for Amazon.com. Through his alumni network, he has identified Jeff, who has been working at Amazon.com as a retail buyer for five years. Mike sends an email request, stating his current position as a student and that he is highly interested in working for Amazon.com. He also sends over his resume so that Jeff can get to know him beforehand. Let's look at the basic building blocks of the informational interview:

Introductions and Intention Statement: This is where you clearly lay out how you want the conversation to play, as well as start off strong by showing that you are really interested in the company and that you have done a lot of preparation and homework prior to the call. It also is a chance to remind the person you are speaking with about your experiences and qualifications (because he probably didn't read the resume you sent him). It is also helpful to take an extra step to find an open job that you want on the company website. That way, if he decides to refer you, you can quickly send him the job that you applied for so that he can find the hiring manager.

Here is what a good introduction and intention statement looks like for Mike.

Jeff, first of all, I really appreciate the time you are taking to speak with me. Like I mentioned in my email, I am really interested in working for Amazon.com, and especially in your particular role. As you know from my resume, I have about four years of working in retail. I feel like Amazon could be a really good fit for my experiences.

In the next thirty minutes, I'd like to get a better understanding of what it would be like working for Amazon.com so that, when I apply for a position I have a better knowledge of the company and, specifically, the retail buying role before I officially apply for the job.

Ask Questions: This is the bulk of the interview, where you can distinguish yourself by showing that you have done your homework and are genuinely interested in the company. But remember that not all questions are created equal. Good questions are general questions that just about anyone at the company can answer, while great questions are specific questions that show that you have put the effort into researching the company. Here are some examples of how to turn a good question into a great one.

Good Question: *What is Amazon trying to accomplish over the long term?*

Great Question: *I know that Amazon's mission is to be the world's most customer-centric organization.*

How does that vision play out in your daily work at Amazon.com? And how is that different from other places you've worked?

Good Question: *What's the work/life balance like at Amazon.com?*

Great Question: *As I've researched the company, I noticed that many employees work really hard at Amazon.com.*

How have you personally been able to balance the demands of work with the demands of your family and other areas of your life?

Good Question: *What types of people are most successful at Amazon.com?*

Great Question: *Amazon's website talks about how people with a bias for action and the ability to dive deep into problems in order to solve them are successful at Amazon.com. Can you talk about some specific examples of how you've seen this come to life in your work and that of your co-workers?*

Ask for resume tips: There is no one better to critique your resume than an employee of your targeted company. This is because they have specific insight into what the company is looking for and can give you tailored insight that will help your resume get selected. It is also yet another chance for the employee to be the expert—and who doesn't want to be an expert?

Ask for help and close: At this point, the interviewee should be feeling pretty good. After all, he has spent the last thirty minutes as the expert and he has the great feeling one gets through helping another. In really good interviews, the employee will offer his assistance in passing along your resume even before you ask. But if not, this is the perfect time to ask.

> *Jeff, thanks again for taking the time to speak with me. This has been very helpful in increasing my understanding of Amazon.com. I started the interview very interested in working for the company. This interview has only increased my interest. I will be applying for a retail buyer position currently posted online. Would you*

> be willing to help me get my application and resume into
> the right hands?

These interviews work. I once had a friend from my alma mater contact me for an informational interview that followed this process. The flow of the conversation was similar to the above example. By the types of questions he was asking, I could tell that he had done his homework and was genuinely interested in the company. By the end of the phone conversations, I had committed to making some phone calls to the right people and to making sure his resume landed in the right hands. This resulted in an internship for him. It was the most productive thirty minutes that this individual spent in job hunting. Such is the power of informational interviewing.

Job hunting is too competitive not to use this simple tool to your advantage. The alternative is to continue to submit your resume online with the other hundreds of people.

Part 2: Nailing the Interview

All the work you have put in thus far has gotten you to this point, and now that work is basically irrelevant. Why? Because resumes don't get you jobs, they get you the interview. Interviews get you the job. Rarely will a hiring manager go back and review resumes after interviewing a group of people for a position. By that time, they have put the candidates through a rigorous interview and there has emerged a clear winner. That's why it is critical that you not rest on your laurels and assume you can just fly through the interview. It does not matter that your resume is the favorite of the bunch before the interview or that you have personal contact with someone inside the company. On the other hand, it doesn't matter if you barely squeaked by the resume screening process and, by some miracle, secured an interview. Either way, the best interviewee will get the job. It's anyone's game at this point.

The way to beat your competition is to out-prepare them. Once you've secured the interview, forget about your resume and focus your full efforts on your interview performance. You should spend ten to twenty hours preparing. This gives you adequate time to research, formulate, and practice. Here is a winning sequence to follow for preparation:

1. **Research:** Conduct general research on the company, position, and, if possible, those interviewing you—twenty percent of your time.

2. **Formulate:** Anticipate interview questions and develop your answers—forty percent of your time.

3. **Practice:** Conduct mock interviews on yourself until you are 100% comfortable—forty percent of your time.

I will discuss each of these preparation stages in great detail. I will also provide you with multiple interview questions and provide you with a structured way to answer them properly. But before we dive into the details, let's first cover the basic structure of an interview, as well as interview decorum and etiquette.

The bulk of corporate interviews are structured to be an hour long, with the interviewer taking forty-five minutes to ask you questions and then giving you fifteen minutes to ask questions. A corporate interview will ask three general types of questions: "get to know you" questions, "behavioral-based questions," and "case questions." A typical sixty-minute interview may be structured as follows:

Get to know you questions—ten minutes: These questions sound like, "Walk me through your resume," or "Why are you applying for this job?" They give the interviewer some insight into who you are and help him make sense of why you want the job. These are "check the box" questions. They are more of a warmup for the meatier questions to come.

Behavioral-based questions—twenty-five minutes: These questions gauge how well you have exhibited certain behaviors in the past and therefore your likelihood to exhibit those behaviors in the future.

Case question—ten minutes: These are hypothetical business situations that allow the interviewer to assess how you solve problems and structure your thinking. These questions easily weed out an under- prepared candidate.

Of course, not all interviews are structured this way. Some companies will require you to complete a written case and present your findings to a group of people. Other companies may require you to complete a personality test. I once met with a psychiatrist as part of my interview process. (He must have diagnosed me as crazy because I did not get the job.)

And then there is basic interview etiquette. The last thing you want is to be put on the "do not hire" list because you violated basic interview decorum principles. Here are some key things to consider:

Dress: You should look your absolute best for the interview. This means business professional—suits and ties for men and suits or formal dresses for women. Some companies, especially technology companies or small start-ups, have a reputation for being more casual. Rarely will dressing in business profession-al attire count against you, but sometimes it can. If you aren't sure, you can always ask the recruiter how you should dress. Unless they tell you specifically that you should wear more ca-sual clothing, you should keep it formal.

Punctuality: Show up for the interview ten to fifteen min-utes early. Being late can be "fashionable" in social situations but, in a business environment, it is just plain rude. If you are traveling to the corporate office and you are not familiar with the location, give yourself plenty of time.

Also, you will likely be given fifteen minutes at the end of the interview to ask your questions. This is an opportunity for you to ask insightful questions and further sell yourself, but do not exceed this time limit. Be respectful of your interviewer's busy schedule by asking the most important two or three questions that you have.

First impressions: When you see your interviewer for the first time, look the interviewer in the eye, greet him or her with a genuine smile and give them a firm handshake. Let them feel your enthusiasm and passion right from the start.

Correspondence: Either the interviewer or the recruiter should tell you at some point when you should expect to hear back from them with the final decision about your candidacy. If they don't volunteer the information, it is perfectly appropriate to ask. If you don't hear back from them by the committed time, it is okay to follow up via email or phone call. It also helps to write a handwritten thank-you note to your interviewers be-tween the interview and the time you hear back. A first-class thank-you note would reiterate your interest in the company, thank them for the time, and demonstrate that you remembered something personal about them.

LET'S PREPARE TO WIN

It's now time to discuss how to use your ten hours of preparation to land the job. If you are not fully persuaded that you should spend at least ten hours preparing for an interview, please join me in a brief visualization exercise.

Envision yourself in an interview for a job that you really, really want. You enter the room, greet the interviewer with a smile, and start to speak about your experiences. You have prepared only a couple of hours for this interview. After all, you are a charismatic person with good experience. As the interviewer asks the questions, you feel reasonably comfortable with the answers you are giving. There aren't any long pauses or things that are extremely difficult. You notice, however, that some of your answers are taking a little longer to get to. You find yourself thinking of the answers and repeating yourself on a few occasions. But this isn't a big deal. The interviewer won't penalize you too much for this. Toward the end of the interview, you ask a few questions and close by thanking him for his time. You walk out of the interview feeling like the interview went well. You also feel like you are qualified to do the job.

Now envision your competition. This is the candidate that enters the room directly after you to interview for the same position. He is asked the same questions and evaluated in the same way. This person is charismatic and has excellent experience—just like you. In fact, this person is like you in every single way—years of experience, leadership ability, and analytical aptitude. The only difference between you and your competitor is that he has taken the time to prepare meticulously for the interview. Because of this, he or she answers every question in a way that fully impresses the hiring manager. There is no rambling. There are no awkward pauses. Every question is answered in a concise and poignant way, and he never repeats himself. In the end, he gets the job.

Let me emphasize again that in this scenario, you are both equally qualified for the position. The difference is that your competition trained for the race; you just simply showed up hoping to get by on your good looks and you got waxed!

Ten to twenty hours may seem like overkill, but it only amounts to one or two typical days of work at the office. If you get the job and stay for five years, you will be working there well over 1,500 days. That's 1,500 days of a job that you want to be at. Or you could lose out and then get a less desirable job because you thought three hours was enough preparation time. That's 1,500 days of a job that you DON'T want to be at. Looking at it in this light, ten hours is a small price to pay in order to ensure you get what you want.

Now it's time to discuss the different elements of preparation and how they can help you specifically:

RESEARCH

In this phase, you are gathering basic information about the company and position. You want to be in a position where you can answer simple questions about the company if asked, or weave your knowledge into the interview. For example, you should never walk into an interview without knowing a company's annual revenue. Other basic information can include the company's main product lines, the name of its CEO, its corporate vision and mission statements, and its primary competitors.

Here is a sampling of helpful resources as you conduct your research:

The Company Website: This will give you a feel for what kind of message the company is sending to its customers and how it wants to be perceived by the public. It should also have the corporate vision and mission statement. If the company is an online company, like Amazon.com or eBay, you should spend the bulk of your time here. It is helpful to think of ways that you would improve the website to enhance the user experience if you were an employee. If you are not a current user of the website, you should become one before walking into the interview.

SEC Filings: The web address to access this is EDGAR.GOV. Enter the company name and you will see the annual (10K) and quarterly (10Q) reports. The most important is the annual report, as this is generally the report with the most commentary about the numbers (just as insightful as the numbers themselves is the story the corporation is telling about them). And you can also access the proxy statements, which will tell you how much the senior executives make if you want to have a little fun or do a little day-dreaming!

Other helpful financial websites are Yahoo!Finance, MSN.com, and MSNBC.com. These sites provided summarized financial statements from the prior five to ten years, as well as Wall Street analysts' opinions about the company. You can also set Google Alerts to email you periodically on the latest company updates.

Current Employees: At this point, you have probably already conducted an informational interview with an employee of the company and this person may even have helped to get you the interview. It is perfectly acceptable to call the employee back, tell him that you have been contacted for an interview, thank him for helping you in the process, and ask some additional questions. The only time it is not okay to call is if this person will be interviewing you or if he or she is directly involved in the hiring decision. Your goal here is to get the inside scoop on how to be successful without making them feel like they are divulging too much information. Here are three good questions to ask:

1. The recruiter has told me that Jane will be interviewing me. Can you give me some insight on how I can be successful in an interview with her?
2. What are the top skills that have made you successful in your position? (This is a great way to get insight into the types of questions you will be asked without having to ask it.)
3. What types of candidates have been successful in interviews, and which types of candidates have not? (Another way of getting insight into the questions that will be asked.)

Past Employees: People who no longer work for the company are especially useful because they have no hidden agenda. While a current employee may want to conceal or sugarcoat, a past employee will have no problem telling it to you straight. It is helpful to know why the person left the company—whether he or she was fired, or just unhappy, or had a better opportunity—to allow you to put their comments in context. You can basically ask this group anything you want and they will likely answer any question you ask!

Interaction with the Product: If possible, figure out a way to use the product or service as a consumer before the interview. This will show that you at least have knowledge of the product from a consumer's point of view. If it is not possible to try the product, read some online reviews or ask some friends. Figure out what is being said about the company on social media.

FORMULATING

Now that you are well versed on the basics of the company and position, you should embark on the intellectual process of anticipating the questions that you will be asked and reflecting on your prior professional and life experience to create compelling answers for the interviewer.

Again, there are three types of questions that will be asked: "Get to know you" questions, "behavioral" questions, and "hypothetical," or "case," questions.

GET TO KNOW YOU QUESTIONS

The first type of questions, the "get to know you" questions, will happen at the beginning of the interview. There is generally just one of these questions, and it sounds something like this:

"Tell me about yourself."

"Walk me through your resume."

"Why are you interested in working for our company?"

"Tell me about how you got to this point?"

Now, let me translate what these questions really mean. If they were saying precisely what they were looking for, they would say "In no more than five minutes, chronologically take me through each experience on your resume, highlighting just the most impressive and relevant parts, doing it in a way that shows you have skills that perfectly match this position, and then tell me why you chose to apply for this job in a way that seems really reasonable and doesn't sound desperate, and then make me feel like my company is the best company on earth and that you really want to work for it—again, in a way that doesn't sound desperate. Oh, and please don't be boring because if you are I won't listen to the last four minutes of your speech."

While this translation is dramatized, it is nonetheless what they are looking for with this opening statement. Prepare accordingly. Basically, these get to know you questions are asking for your opening statement. A great opening statement must include three things: first, good experience neatly summarized; second, high-level results; and third, a logical reason for applying for the job. Here is an example of how to craft your opening statement. If you are just out of college, you can highlight your coursework and even craft any part-time work that may be relevant.

Suppose Leah, who is just getting out of college, is applying for a job as a sales representative with Hewlett-Packard. A good opening statement for her would sound something like this:

> Thank you for taking the time to interview me. Let me take you through my resume and talk about why I am interested in working in the technology industry and, specifically, Hewlett-Packard. Growing up, I always had a

fascination for and interest in technology. I took every opportunity in high school to be around computers. I found that, while I was good at working with computers, I was actually better at explaining how they worked to others. In fact, I was paid in high school several times to help set up home computers for my friends' parents, as well as train them on how to use them. (This last sentence shows relevant interest, experience, and implied results. If you were getting paid to do this, you clearly had a knack for it.)

When I started college, I needed something to pay the bills, and so I took a job with Best Buy (more relevant experience) as a sales analyst on the floor. This allowed me to use my knack for explaining computers and taught me a lot more about the products (more relevant experience). In fact, in my second year, I wound up being the top salesperson in my store and I have stayed in the top ten percent of salespeople until the present time (strong results).

I chose to major in marketing and sales so that I could hone my ability to work with people and sell. I joined the sales club at my university and pushed the club to put more emphasis on technology sales. I even formed a group that met bi-monthly to discuss sales careers in the technology industry (more relevant experience and interest).

During my work at Best Buy and in my coursework, I learned a lot about HP products and gained a passion for them (interest in the company). I believe I could be a great ambassador for HP as a salesperson. I understand each product's advantages and have been successful at selling them for three years now (more implied results). I am really interested in working for HP and look forward to answering any other questions that you have.

If you are a more seasoned businessperson, you can follow the same pattern. Talk about your experiences in the context of the current position, show that you have results, and then talk about why you are applying for the position.

Location can also be to your advantage here. If you really want to live where your company is located, you should make that clear. This will give the employer confidence that you would accept the job if you were given an offer.

BEHAVIORAL-BASED QUESTIONS

Now on to the behavioral-based questions. These types of questions are the most popular of interview questions and generally take up most of the interview time. The rationale for corporations using these questions is that if a candidate can succinctly point to examples in their past experience where they have demonstrated a desired behavior, then they are likely to demonstrate that same desired behavior in future. The magic in these questions is in the requirement to cite specific examples, rather than generalities. To ensure this specificity, the questions start with the phrase, "Tell me about a time when..." Hence, answering this question in generalities really doesn't answer the question. You *must* be specific.

Imagine for a moment that you are selling your house and you are interviewing a realtor to decide if you will hire them. You specifically want to know how good they are at preparing a house to look "show-ready." One question you might ask is "How good are you at preparing houses to sell?" To this, the realtor could respond, "I am really good at it." This won't be helpful to you at all. Or, you could ask a better question: "What is your approach to getting a house ready?" This would give you some more detail about their approach, but this still is an inferior question because you don't know that this realtor actually follows this approach. You may get a great-sounding answer but you won't have any assurance that the answer is true. Finally, you could ask, "Tell me about the last home you sold. What was your specific approach to preparing the home for sale, and what happened as a result?" This is an excellent question. Now the candidate has to demonstrate in very specific terms how he has the skills to successfully prepare a home for sale. Only by asking a question about past behavior will you get an accurate answer.

It is the same with corporate interviews. If the company is looking for, say, analytical ability, the recruiter will ask about a specific time when you demonstrated that analytical ability.

Behavioral-based questions can vary greatly in wording—there can literally be hundreds of variations. This can be extremely overwhelming. But despite the variation in how the questions are asked, there are usually only four or five core skills they are trying to assess. The key is to practice enough that you develop the ability to detect patterns and understand what they are asking.

Here are the most popular skills businesses seek to assess, with some examples of questions they ask:

- **Leadership:** Tell me about a time when you...
  - Led a team through a difficult business challenge.
  - Led a team to accomplish an important objective.
  - Went against the common consensus for an initiative in which you deeply believed.

- Had to make a tough decision that you felt was the right thing to do.
- Had to motivate a team that had previously been unmotivated.
- **Analytical Ability:** Tell me about a time when you...
  - Managed a complex project.
  - Used your critical thinking skills to solve a business problem.
  - Took something complicated and made it simple.
  - Used your brain to think through a problem involving numbers.
  - Used numbers to persuade someone on your team.
- **Strategic Thinking:** Tell me about a time when you...
  - Created a business strategy for a business that was declining.
  - Conducted an assessment of a business model.
  - Thought through how your product was different from that of a competitor.
  - Put together a cohesive action plan for your boss.
- **Working Well With Others:** Tell me about a time when you...
  - Had a difficult boss or co-worker and yet still had to develop a strong working relationship.
  - Had a challenging person on your team that was hindering your team's progress.
  - Had to persuade someone to your way of thinking.
  - Had to admit that you were wrong.
- **Drive for Results:** Tell me about a time when you...
  - Exceeded the expectations placed on you.

- • Missed a critical business objective. How did you react?
- • **Business Savvy:** Tell me about a time when you...
  - • Noticed a business trend that you knew was going to have an impact on your business.
  - • Used your brain to make some quick money in your personal life.
  - • Had to cut costs in your own household.

The actual list of questions can get quite large. But do not get overwhelmed. While the list of questions is large, the list of skills being assessed is small. Many of these questions are just different ways of asking the same thing. For example, if a company is looking for leadership skills, the recruiter may ask, "Tell me about a time when you had to lead a team," or "Tell me about a time when you had to make a difficult decision that affected other employees," or they may ask, "Tell me about a time when you had someone who worked for you who had lost motivation to work hard." While these questions sound different, they are all trying to assess the same thing—leadership. And just because there may be twenty different ways of asking a leadership question doesn't mean that you have to develop twenty separate responses. You only need one or two really strong examples of leadership and then to position your answers slightly differently, depending on the exact question you are asked.

With practice, answering these questions can become easy. There is a proven method used in the business world to tackle these types of questions. It is commonly referred to as the

STAR method of answering interview questions. It follows this format:

- **S**ituation: Set up the business context of your response. Make it clear and simple. Don't take too much time and don't bog them down with confusing industry details or context.
- **T**ask: Tell them the task you needed to complete. You don't need to give a lot of detail here, either. Just state your challenge.
- **A**ction: What did you specifically do in order to demonstrate this skill? This is where you should spend most of your time.
- **R**esult: What happened after you took the action and what effect did it have?

Given that you have already researched this company and position, you should have a directional feel for which three to five skills it will seek to assess. To save time and stress guessing which exact questions you will be asked, the best thing for you to do is reflect on your past work experience and create one great example for each skill. That is five stories to seven stories (if you want a couple of backups). That's it! That is certainly better than trying to guess which of the fifty questions they will ask you.

Also, remember that your responses should be at least three, but no more than five, minutes long. And the bulk of your response should focus on the "A" portion of the STAR framework, where you describe the specific things you did to solve the problem. It's all about YOU and why YOU are a rock star!

HYPOTHETICAL, OR "CASE," QUESTIONS

The case question is perhaps the most difficult interview question to answer and therefore the most feared of all interview questions. My intent is to give you some exposure to these questions and teach you a very broad and simple way of thinking about them. I will not make you a case question master in this chapter but I will take some of the mystique out of the process. Then you can take this information and practice until you feel comfortable answering them yourself.

The purpose of the case question is to assess how a candidate thinks—how he or she approaches a problem which they have never encountered. Unlike behavioral-based questions, which seek to determine how someone would act in a particular situation, case questions seek to answer how a candidate would think.

Case questions are not about the "right" answer. The right answer to a case question doesn't exist. Rather, answering a case question well demonstrates your ability to think through business issues in a logical way and then articulate your thinking in a manner that is persuasive. Hence, like so many other things in business, it's not about being right; it's about sounding like you know what you are talking about.

90% of case questions can be answered in about five to seven minutes and do not require a pen and paper, although you may use one to jot down a few thoughts and calculations if you'd like. Simplicity and logical structure are the key ingredients here.

Here is a sampling of case questions that could be asked in an interview:

Business problem/Strategic thinking

- You are the CEO of Hewlett-Packard, and most of your business is in the declining PC segment. What do you do to fix this problem and return the company to growth?

- You are the brand manager for Clorox and a new competitor just came into the market with a new bleach product at a lower price. As the business leader, what do you do in order to combat this?

- Suppose we hired you into our company, what are the three things you would do on your first week to get up to speed on the business?

- You manage a fast food restaurant and are asked by corporate to cut costs in order to grow profit. How would you go about doing this?

Leadership situation

- Suppose you lead a team of financial analysts. One of your employees really struggles with some key financial concepts that are critical to completing the job. What do you do?

- How do you deal with a really high performer who you both agree should be promoted but you know promotions aren't going to be allowed at the company for at least another year?

- You have just developed a new shoe for Nike and believe that it will be the next big seller for the company. How do you go about getting all the necessary people in the organization "on board" and supporting the launch of this product?

These two types of questions can be answered using a little bit of creativity.

1. Articulate the problem and its implications: Re-stating the problem to ground yourself and the interviewer never hurts. Case questions can be confusing at first, so it never hurts to start out stating your purpose. Also, you can expand on the problem to talk about what it means in a given circumstance.

2. In this case, you state the overriding principle of what you are trying to solve and tell the interviewer how you are going to solve it. This reassures the interviewer that you understand the question and that you are trying to articulate it further.

3. Generate and evaluate options: This is the most important part of the answer. Before diving into an answer, take them through your thinking by generating the options. Then—and most importantly—spend a little time evaluating each option, one at a time. If there is an area where candidates shoot themselves in the foot, it's here. They shoot off as many options as they can and spend little to no time evaluating the options. Yet it's in the evaluating that your real thinking prowess is demonstrated.

4. Make a recommendation: Throughout your answer, it's okay to ask a clarifying question or two. It's also okay to

make some assumptions about things you don't know. Employees of real businesses make assumptions all the time. Simply call out that you are making an assumption and move forward.

Creative thinking

- Take a look at this pen. Give me five different ways that it can be positioned to sell in the marketplace.
- What is some of the best advertising that you've seen lately and why was it so good?
- Last year, the Crayola company launched a new crayon that is neon yellow and didn't sell well in the market. We now have a huge surplus of this crayon and none of our current customers want to buy it. How would you help us recoup some of the costs?

Quantitative Conundrum

- How many pounds does a fully loaded 747 passenger airplane weigh?
- How much coal can a mile-long Union Pacific freight train carry?
- You manage a high-end hotel in New York City 250 rooms, each equipped with pay-per-view televisions, and three restaurants that also provide room service. What percent of revenue do you think comes from room fees vs. food vs. purchased TV shows?

Complex case questions: A small number of companies will give you more complex case questions. The top consulting firms are notorious for this. These questions come in written form and require a written and oral presentation after a thirty-minute or more preparation period. The techniques discussed in this chapter will certainly apply to those types of questions as well but the actual rigor of the question may be harder. These questions are no joke. To master the questions, I recommend working closely with your university career services or reading some additional books that focus on consulting case questions.

FINAL QUESTIONS

Finally, toward the end of the interview, you will be given about fifteen minutes to ask questions. There is usually only time to ask one or two questions and it is important to be respectful of the interviewer's time, so make sure you don't ask questions when the time is up unless the interviewer gives you the OK.

Make no mistake, the purpose of these questions to the interviewer is to make you look interested and smart. Forget about asking about pay and work/life balance—those can be asked *after* you get the job. No matter how well you think you did in the interview, you haven't been offered the job yet, so consider the last couple of questions that you ask an opportunity for you to seal the deal.

Chapter Summary

1. In today's low-loyalty environment, job-landing skills will serve you well throughout your entire career.

2. There are two primary components to getting a job today:

   a. Getting the interview

      i. Ensure you have a resume that incorporates the Four Rs.

         1. Readability: The format and verbiage should be simple and flawless.

         2. Relevance: Your experience relates to the job at hand. If it does not relate directly, then bridge the language to show that your prior experience can translate to your future job.

         3. Responsibility: It clearly shows what your scope of responsibility was at your prior employers. The best way to do this is through a responsibility statement.

         4. Results: It has clear and quantifiable results.

      ii. Use the power of informational interviews to get your resume pulled from the pile.

   b. Nailing the interview

      i. Out-prepare your competition by:

         1. Researching the prospective company via online searches and current or past employees.

         2. Formulating your answers

a. Three types of questions

  i. "Get to know you" questions: This is where you concisely show that you are highly qualified and highly interested in the job.

  ii. Behavioral-based questions: Get five excellent stories that demonstrate skills that the company is looking for. Use the STAR method.

  iii. Case questions: restate, evaluate options, and offer recommendations with logic.

4. Practicing until you know them cold

ii. When given the opportunity, ask two to three questions that show that you have thought deeply about the job and are highly interested in the job.

9

SKILL #8: BALANCING–DON'T HATE YOUR LIFE

GREW UP VISITING MY GRANDPARENT'S CABIN IN SOUTHWEST Montana every summer. The property sits just a few hundred feet from a pristine mountain lake containing ice-cold water filled with rainbow trout. Each summer, I filled my days with fishing, boating, motorcycling, and waterskiing. These fun-filled days in Montana served as an escape from the modern, media-saturated suburban life that I was accustomed to back home in California. The cabin was equipped with a landline telephone that made local calls only. When I wanted to communicate with friends in California, I wrote letters. When my siblings and I wanted to entertain ourselves at night, we played games or read books. Perhaps some would have called our way of life at the cabin primitive and uninformed. But I found it a very peaceful, deliberate way to live during the summer.

I still visit the cabin every summer, now with my wife and children. The picturesque and pristine mountain landscape is the same as it was twenty-five years ago. The lake is still ice cold and full of gorgeous rainbow trout. The only thing that has changed over the last twenty years is our behavior while visiting. It is not uncommon for my siblings and me to be gathered together in the great room with the fire crackling. Yet, instead of playing games together, each of us is captivated by our own virtual world brought to us by separate mobile devices. Sometimes one of us is taking a work call in another room or digitally streaming a movie that has just been released. The access to the outer world that wouldn't have been possible at the cabin just twenty years prior is now commonplace. While I love the convenience my phone provides at the cabin, part of me mourns the death of a simpler, less distracting life. There seems to be no escape to our electronically connected lives, even in the mountains of Southwest Montana.

This technology shift has changed not only our vacation behavior but also our approach to work. Twenty-five years ago, it simply wasn't possible to check email while attending your daughter's soccer game or take a conference call while running errands. But today it's not only possible, it's commonplace and even expected at times. Every corporate boss knows that no employee is truly "unavailable" or "without service."

Over the last several decades, US labor productivity has increased exponentially. Through the wonders of technology and innovation, the average US worker in 2016 was 4.3 times more productive than the average worker was in 1947[11]. This means that an employee today could work less than one-fourth of the hours than someone in 1947 and achieve the same output. Even over the last ten years, productivity has increased by

---

11 Bureau of Labor Statistics, *Productivity Change in the Nonfarm Business Sector*, 1947-2016

twenty-five percent. Yet have you noticed anyone taking advantage of this phenomenon by reducing the number of hours they are working? Me neither.

Today, people are not working less; rather, they are working slightly more. According to one study by the Center for American Progress, the number of professional men working fifty hours per week or more went from thirty-four percent in 1977 to thirty-eight percent in 2008. And the number of professional women working fifty hours per week or more went from six percent to nearly fifteen percent over the same time. Americans, it seems, aren't slowing down any time soon.

There is no doubt that technology has been a major contributing factor to our productivity gains. It has raised the standard of living for millions across the globe. Personal computers, mobile devices, and the internet are tools that multiply our ability to create and consume information. But the irony of these productivity-enabling devices is that they are also the root cause of our increased work hours. In one survey of employed email users conducted in 2008, fifty percent of respondents reported that they checked work email on the weekends, forty-six percent checked work email on sick days, and thirty-four percent checked work email while on vacation.[12]

As our ability to connect from anywhere has increased, we have seen the rise of the modern-day workaholic. Of course, workaholics have been around for ages, but today's workaholic is a different creature. Unlike pre-email and pre-cellphone workaholics, whose long hours in the office made it so they

---

12 Pew Research Center 's Internet and American Life Project. "Networked Workers Study 2008"

couldn't deny their workaholism, the modern-day workaholic can live in a high-functioning state of denial, attending sports games and doing other activities while still taking conference calls and shooting off emails. They can seemingly "do it all" and "be everywhere." Rather than deal with a cold office in the late hours of the night, the modern-day workaholic has the option to work himself to death within the comforts of his own home.

Of course, hard work is essential to success in corporate America. Indeed, to be competitive, you will be required to put in diligent, focused work for your employer. But there is a difference between working hard and working too much. The former is productive, while the latter can be destructive. Consistently pushing oneself beyond your limits and not implementing balance has unpleasant consequences. Multiple studies[13] have concluded that working long hours (55+ per week) increases the risk of heart disease, depression, anxiety, and premature death. According to this data, working to death is more than just a clever phrase.

Not only do physical and mental health suffer when one works too much but productivity suffers as well. An article titled "Working Too Much, Get a Life," published in *Economist*

---

13 1) Worked to Death? A census-based longitudinal study of the relationship between the number of hours spent working and mortality risk by Dermott O'Reilly and Michael Monsanto, 2) Long working hours and symptoms of anxiety and depression: a 5 year follow-up of the Whitewall 2 study. M. V M. Virtanen[a1 c1], J. E. Ferrie[a2], A. Singh-Manoux[a2a3a4], M. J. Shipley[a2], S. A. Stansfeld[a5], M. G. Marmot[a2], K. Ahola[a1], J. Vahtera[a1a6a7] and M. Kivimäki[a2.] 3) Long Working Hours and Coronary Heart Disease: A Systematic Review and Meta-Analysis, Marianna Virtanen[*], Katriina Heikkilä, Markus Jokela, Jane E. Ferrie, G. David Batty, Jussi Vahtera and , Mika Kivimäki

magazine[14] shows a chart on the negative correlation between productivity and long working hours. The chart gathered multiple data points from a group of countries with modern economies. The data is clear: Each additional hour worked shows a decreasing rate of productivity.

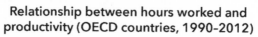

Relationship between hours worked and productivity (OECD countries, 1990-2012)

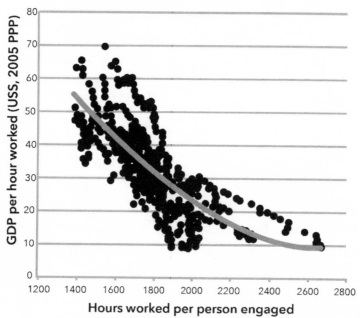

Most people I've encountered who work long hours admit that they work too much. They also admit that they aren't happy about it. They see the inherent value in the often-repeated phrase, "Nobody wishes on their death bed that they had spent more time in the office," but they can't seem to translate what they believe into daily practice. Many feel trapped by the ex-

14 "Proof that you should get a life," *Economist*, Dec 9th 2014

ternal pressures around them, and helpless to break free from them. Often they blame their circumstances. Common statements like "If only my boss wasn't so demanding" or "If my job didn't have such tight deadlines" or "If my co-workers didn't work so many hours then I wouldn't feel so guilty for leaving the office before dinner," serve as excuses for continuing in their unhealthy and unhappy lifestyle. These and many other reasons are valid and understandable challenges. But, alas, they are just reasons; they are not solutions.

I deeply empathize with those who feel the immense pressure to work longer and harder. I have, many times, succumbed to the external pressures to overwork. This pressure has caused me to work late into the night, work early in the mornings, and put in time on Saturdays. The pressures of my job have, at times, woken me up in the middle of the night and even affected my physical health. I have experienced for myself the negative effect overworking can have on my health, my mental state, and my family.

So, if so many of us know that working too much is detrimental to so many aspects of our lives, why do we do it? What is our motivation? I have concluded from my personal experience, observation, and interviews with other corporate employees that there are four basic human motivations that drive one to overwork. These motivations are survival, gain, self-worth, and passion.

Personal gain: These individuals are motivated by money, power, authority, status, or glory. They keep their eye on the prize and it drives them forward to work longer and harder than their competition. They are able to justify the sacrifice they make in other areas on their lives because the reward is worth it to them.

Survival: These individuals operate with a fear of loss: loss of a job; loss of a promotion; loss of status or reputation. They are trying to "keep their head above water" and believe that the extra hours are the best way to accomplish that.

Self-worth: Many attach who they are to what they do. If they aren't excelling at their jobs, they think they aren't excelling at life. These people are highly competitive with themselves and with others. To these people, working long hours and sacrificing makes them feel good about themselves.

Passion: These people genuinely love what they do. They take great satisfaction and pride in their work. These are the lucky ones; they have found what they love to do and are doing it every day. But even passion, although probably the noblest of the four motivations, can be taken to an unhealthy extreme.

Workaholism stems from one of those four basic motivations or some combination of the four motivations. What's more, motivation can evolve over time. For example, you may not realize that you are motivated by money until you are offered a lucrative promotion that will require a more demanding schedule. Other people don't realize how much they care about job survival until a round of layoffs scares them into 70 hours per week.

The point of laying out these motivations is not to persuade you to ditch all motivation. There is value in each of these motivations, to a certain extent. It is not a sin to make a little money nor is it a crime to attach some level of self-esteem to your profession. The challenge is when it pushes workers to imbalance, causing other vital parts of life—physical health, spirituality, community involvement—to suffer.

The fact that working too much is unhealthy is easily understandable. But what's often counterintuitive is that working extra hours is often unnecessary to reach one's goals. There are multiple examples of people who have made a lot of money, survived in their jobs, maintained great self-esteem and fulfilled their passions without being thrown completely out of balance. It is possible to get what you want without ruining your life.

Not only is it possible to achieve balance while satisfying your motivations, but enforcing balance in your daily schedule is the most probable way to reach your loftiest ambitions. Balance creates the resilience that allows you to bounce back from failure or setbacks.

Myths of Balance

Before we get into the solutions that help promote work-life balance, let's look at some of the fake solutions that don't work. Real solutions involve really tough decisions, while fake solutions usually involve denial and "business as usual" behavior. People attempt to solve problems without making difficult decisions. They mask their problem, providing some illusion of progress and giving mental comfort in the short term, but never fix the root causes. Before real solutions can be learned and internalized, the fake solutions must be recognized and ejected from your mindset.

There are three primary fake solutions to achieving work-life balance:

Multitasking: It is difficult to find a job description today that doesn't require the "ability to multitask" as a core job skill.

Corporate culture is obsessed with multitasking. Instead of expecting employees to focus on accomplishing a task well, they are expected to accomplish multiple tasks well simultaneously.

Unfortunately, the human brain doesn't work that way. In 1999, Stanford Professor Clifford Nass ran a study on those who considered themselves "high-tech jugglers" or, in other words, people who preferred to check email, watch TV, surf the internet, and perform other electronic tasks simultaneously. He ran cognitive tests on these individuals and compared the results to low electronic multi-taskers, those that preferred to accomplish one task at a time. The tests deliberately included several distractions along the way. The study found that the high multi-taskers turned out to be "suckers for irrelevancy" and had trouble separating the elements that were relevant to complete the test from the distractions. The low multi-taskers, on the other hand, had less trouble ignoring those things that were irrelevant to their tasks and were better at storing and organizing the information necessary to successfully complete the test. The paradoxical conclusion: by doing less, people accomplish more.

Work harder: This fake solution assumes that if you don't have enough time to get the work done, you should just put your head down and grind it out a little more.

This method could potentially work for someone who is lazy and performing at a very low level. But most people at your company aren't lazy. Neither are you. To tell someone who is already working hard to just work harder is like telling the driver of a car that is stuck in the mud to apply additional power to the gas pedal. Those who try to work harder as a solution eventually "run themselves into the ground," digging an even deeper pit for themselves. And, by working harder and harder, they have set the expectation for their employer that they have superhuman strength and capacity beyond normal mortals. The next time a deadline comes up, the company will expect them to work at the same breakneck pace and get even more done. The pit keeps getting deeper. It never stops.

Just give it three more years: This is probably the most dangerous of all the fake solutions. It is a procrastination tool used by many to kick their work-life balance problem down the road like an irresponsible politician would pass a budget problem to his successor. The statements made by those who use this fake solution usually sound like this: "I know my work-life balance is terrible right now, but if I can just get through these next three years, I will..." and then comes one or more of the following statements:

- Be in a financial position where I can focus more on balance
- Be promoted and be able to set my own schedule
- Spend more time with my children
- Make my spouse my number one priority
- Exercise more
- Take time to develop a hobby
- Spend more time serving in my community
- Re-connect with old friends
- Take some time off to relax

Three years is the perfect number for those using this fake solution because it's close enough to trick themselves into thinking they are *actually* going to change their work-life balance, but far enough away to not have to deal with the decision in the foreseeable future.

This thinking is grossly flawed. Granted, after three years, many individuals do get promoted and are indeed in a better financial position than they were before. Those promotions, however, don't come with more freedom over their schedules. Rather, they are accompanied by increased pressure to perform. Instead of relaxation, they get handed more responsibility. Instead of free time, they get more employees to manage. Their reaction to this increased money and responsibility is usually to reset the clock for another three years. And then another, and another, until thirty years have gone by and they wake up and realize that their whole careers that have been chasing after a better balance after "the next three years."

Throw these fake solutions out of your vocabulary, and let's move on to the real solutions.

Internalizing Your Responsibility

Henry Paulsen, the former US Secretary of the Treasury, spent his career with the prestigious investment bank, Goldman Sachs. The investment banking industry, and particularly Goldman Sachs, is known for its extremely long work hours. Yet Henry Paulson, while his kids were young, was able to leave the office at 4:30 pm every day. This allowed him to be home for dinner and read to his children at night. Sure, after his kids were asleep, he would put in some more time at home at night, but he was able to achieve the balance he desired. Later on in his life, when his former employees heard about his schedule, they chided him for working his employees so hard when he was able to be home for dinner. His response: "It's not your boss's job to figure out your life."[15]

In my first corporate job, I remember occasionally staying until 7 pm or so in the office. Every time I would stay in the office, one of my co-workers—I'll call him James—would be there. He was one of many senior managers who worked for the company but the only one who would work those hours. He was a very good employee of the company and a strong performer. I remember thinking that James must have had an unfair workload. The company must have been pressuring him to stay those hours. I felt bad for him until he left the company and someone else (I'll call her Lucy) took his place. Lucy had the same responsibilities as James and came to be a well-respected and top-performing employee, just as James had been. Yet Lucy did not work the same hours as James. She left the office around 5:30 pm every day. Watching the vast difference between James and Lucy taught me an important lesson. The longer work hours by James and the regular work hours by Lucy was not a function of workload—they both had the same responsibilities. Rather, it was a function of the individual choices that James and Lucy made as it related to work-life balance.

While there are several examples of those who have achieved incredible success in their career by obsessing over corporate aspirations only, there are also several examples of people who

---

15 Paulson, Henry, *On the Brink: Inside the Race to Stop the Collapse of the Global Financial System.* Hachette Book Group, New York, NY

have succeeded at work and other areas of life. You can achieve great career success and life success simultaneously. Work and life do not have to be in direct competition. But in order for that to be a reality for you, you will have to deeply internalize that the responsibility for balance rests solely with you. Your company will never say "No" should you decide to work extra hours. There will never be anyone patrolling the corporate halls telling you to go home and see your family, or have fun with your friends, or get some exercise. It is entirely up to you to decide your boundaries. There is no consultant who can make those very personal choices for you. You can always blame your poor work-life balance on something, but blaming does not bring balance. Only accepting the responsibility and challenge for yourself and then taking the necessary corrective measures will bring you the balance that you know you need.

I recognize that this is easier said than done. Clearly, corporations expect strong, productive performance from their employees. Furthermore, some industries demand more hours from their employees than others. For example, consulting and banking jobs typically expect more working hours than most other industries. But, even in the most demanding careers where burn-out is common, it is still possible to achieve a sustainable balance to keep you productive and happy. And work-life balance should be a major factor for you to consider as you choose an industry.

The Work-Life Balance Framework

Work-life balance is highly personal to the individual and thus has no single definition. While one person may think he is achieving an excellent work-life balance by working sixty hours a week instead of eighty, another wouldn't be satisfied unless he had a forty-hour-a-week job. Still others may want to be able to work from home once a week and leave the office once and a while to take care of kids' school activities. The first exercise for you, then, is to define what work-life balance means to you.

When people are looking for an approach to achieve balance, they are often looking for a starting point to get back on track. What they really need is a way of thinking about balance that is different from the way they had been thinking previously. They need to ask themselves three questions and act on the answers.

QUESTION 1: WHAT ARE YOUR DEEPEST VALUES?

This question enables you to think about what you care most about. Write down the things that you value the most. To help facilitate this, think about all the elements of your life and the role you play within each element. Some examples are your spouse or significant other, your children, your freedom, your involvement in the community, your individuality, your friends, your professional career, your lifelong dreams, and your financial stability. Once you have your core values written down, rank them in order of importance.

This task will be difficult if you are doing it right. After all, it's easy to rattle off a series of things that you care about, but it's another thing to list your absolute deepest values and then rank them in order of importance. It should push you to go beyond the surface and examine your true motives in life. For example, you might *say* you value good employment; but good employment is not a deeply held value. Rather, your underlying value might be feeling secure in your job, or feeling useful. Good employment is what you seek in order to satisfy your deeper held value.

QUESTION 2: HOW MUCH TIME DO YOU ALLOCATE TO YOUR TOP VALUES?

Write down the average number of hours per week that you spend on each value. For example, if your first value was family, how many hours a day do you spend with them? Or, if a strong community is important to you, how much time are you spending to make that strong community a reality?

Be practical as you go through this. For example, just because your family may be more important than your work doesn't mean you need to spend more time with them than at work. But if you deeply value family, and you are out the door before your kids wake up and back after your kids go to bed, you are likely not being true to your values. The same goes with exercise, travel, or anything else. Use your judgment to determine the optimal amount of time spent on each value and then be honest with yourself about whether or not you are hitting the mark.

QUESTION 3: WHAT THREE ACTIONS, IF TAKEN, WOULD GET ME CLOSEST TO BETTER LIVING MY CORE VALUES?

If you have determined through Question 2 that your weekly schedule perfectly aligns with your value system, then you can stop and congratulate yourself. But it is more than likely that you have discovered some areas for improvement. To keep it simple, pick three things that will have the biggest impact on your life. These changes do not have to be ground-breaking. One of my personal favorite changes for me in the past was to get up when the alarm clock went off without hitting the snooze button. This enabled me to start the day off in a more deliberate, controlled manner and set the tone for the rest of my day. It was very simple but had a huge impact on helping me be true to myself.

Once you have the three things you need to improve your balance, set specific goals. Make them easy to measure. Set check-ins for yourself periodically. Once you feel you have made the changes and put them into habits, revisit the three questions and get three additional areas of change. The process can be done continuously until you feel that you have achieved the balance you want in life. In other words, you are truly living the life you want to live—with no regrets!

EXECUTIONAL TIPS

You have now created a game plan by asking yourself some tough questions and you've selected three key things that you'd like to change in order to live more in harmony with your values. Now the real challenge comes into play. Once you create rules for yourself, there will be ample opportunities to break them by giving in to the daily pressures at work. You may, for example, decide as part of your plan that you will be home for dinner at least four out of the five workdays. This plan may be going well for the first three days until you are hit with a major deadline. Or, perhaps you are sitting in a meeting that is running past the allotted time and, while you know you need to be heading home, the fact that your boss is still there makes you feel awkward about leaving. Or, you may decide to spend some time at the golf course two Saturdays a month, but one Friday night you receive an email from your boss that has an urgent tone to it and you know that she wants you to "take care of it ASAP." Regardless of what the challenge is, there is no doubt that your plan to implement balance in your life will be challenged in some way or another. Here are some tactics to help you respond to this pressure.

Learn to say "No": People of all personality types don't like to say "No" to others, even when they know they should. Some are born pleasers and hate to disappoint others. Other people are passive in nature and want to avoid uncomfortable confrontations at all costs. Others still are so intensely competitive that they equate saying "No" to a form of weakness or failure.

Regardless of motive, it is a fact that many corporate employees take on more than they should. And while arbitrarily accepting requests may avoid short-term discomfort or confrontation make you feel like you are progressing in your career, it will not help you stay balanced in the long term. Chronic "yes" men or women eventually wind up taking on too much and they pay the price in their personal lives.

There are multiple ways to push back on requests without actually saying no. Here they are:

1. *Ask for the logic behind the request:* Say something like, "You know I always want to help...but can you help me understand the source of this request?"

2. *Put the request in the context of other priorities*: This is especially helpful when your boss is asking something of you in which you feel will put you over the edge. You can start a prioritization conversation like this. "Currently, you've asked me to work on X, Y, and Z, which I believe are all important assignments. This new request is also clearly important, but I don't have the capacity right now to do this new assignment and keep my old assignments according to the prioritization we agreed to? Can you help me understand which item should be deprioritized so that I can take on this new assignment?" This response will help force a conversation about priorities and enable your boss to help manage your workload. He or she may even take the new request off the table after you've served up a reminder of everything else on your plate.

3. *Highlight the implications of the request:* "Okay, I think I understand what you are asking for. Generally, a request like this would take two hours to complete. So I want to make sure that you will need all the data you are asking for vs. just a subset of it."

4. *Narrow the scope of the request:* This technique takes the tactic to an entirely different level. Many times, after you explain to someone the time involved, they are surprised and often narrow the scope of the request. "No, no, I don't want you to spend two hours on this," they might say. "I actually just need X and not the rest." If they don't narrow the scope for you, you can ask some additional questions to make sure you understand the

core of what they are looking for. And if they don't narrow the scope for you, you can always suggest it.

These responses create candid conversations that can drive clarity and save you hours of wasted time. But you must not get pushed around in order to drive them effectively.

Keep commitments to yourself first: There is a reason why airlines tell you in pre-flight that, should oxygen become scarce in the cabin, you should put the oxygen mask on yourself first and your children second. Of course, our natural desire would be to make sure our children are taken care of first but, in a low-oxygen situation, we may not be coherent long enough to take care of anyone. You should—indeed, you must— take care of yourself first so that you can function well enough to take care of others.

It is obvious how this applies to corporations. Keeping commitments to yourself enables you to better keep commitments to others. Virtually everyone would agree that making and keeping commitments to your co-workers is a core part of daily operations at large corporations. When you say you will do something, you do it. If you don't think you will be able to do it, you don't commit to it or you ask for more time or you find the appropriate way to say "No." And yet, while most employees are good at keeping commitments to their co-workers, they have no problem discarding important commitments they have made to *themselves* in favor of "fire drills" or "urgent" requests. For example, you may have made a commitment to yourself that on Fridays you will be out of the office by 5 pm, and yet when your boss asks for something at 4:30 pm, that commitment is easily discarded and you wind up breaking a personal commitment without thinking about it.

If you desire balance in your life, routinely breaking personal commitments is unacceptable. Just imagine if you were to invert this behavior—that you made personal desires the priority and were happy to flake on work commitments to satisfy them. For example, suppose that you have committed to your boss that you would lead an important inter-departmental meeting every Thursday afternoon. The first Thursday rolls around and you decide that you would rather visit the spa, so you blow off the meeting as a result. Such behavior would be considered absurd by your company and may even be grounds for termination. But this is exactly what so many do to their personal lives. Something comes up and they abandon their plans and submit to other's desires.

Occasionally, duty calls and you have to stay late to get something done. And I recognize that many jobs have a culture of company first. You may have to make very modest commitments to yourself to start and even give extra time and effort in other ways. For example, if you want to be home every day for dinner, you may have to come to the office thirty minutes early every day, or put in a few hours every Saturday morning. The point is that *you* are in control.

Ongoing communication with your boss about your personal commitments is critical here. The more your boss knows your desires, the more he or she can try to respect those boundaries and help you keep your commitments.

It's not about working out or going to the movies or whatever, it's about you feeling empowered to execute your plan. It's about taking control of your own decisions and your own balance.

Figure out what works for you: I distinctly remember a time in my career when I was completely exhausted. Business demands were piling up, while at the same time the trends in my business were worsening. I felt trapped underneath a pile of rocks and every day it seemed like one additional rock was added. I couldn't seem to get out from under it. My first reaction to this was to fight back. I would try to work harder and beat it. As a result, I deprioritized other areas of my life to focus more on work. Surely, if I could just get through a few weeks alive, things would get better.

Bad assumption.

When things didn't get better, I began to be angry with the lack of results I was seeing. I was putting in extra effort at work and I felt like I should have been seeing results commensurate with that effort. But nothing changed, and I was starting to fume. After the anger came bitterness. And then came perhaps the most dangerous emotion of all—apathy. And finally, with that apathy came depression. When business leaders asked me questions, I would give the general answers, but I simply had stopped caring. I had lost the fire.

As I was in this apathetic and quasi-depressed state, my energy level was extremely low. I figured that adjusting my sleep habits would help. But more sleep didn't remedy the kind of fatigue that I was feeling. Nor did taking breaks or slowing down help. I just couldn't get out of the funk I was in, regardless of what I tried.

Then I actually tried something that I really, really didn't want to do. I realized that in all my efforts to accelerate my performance, I had become more sedentary and stopped exercising. It seemed odd at first that I would try to cure my lack of drive by expending more energy versus conserving it, but I gave it a try. I decided to commit myself to exercising four to five times per week, 20 minutes each time. I would be dogged about it. I wouldn't let anything get in the way of my exercise schedule.

When I started, I noticed an almost immediate difference that built as I continued my program. I started to sleep more restfully. My appetite increased. I felt better about myself and more in control of my choices. With all this came a more positive outlook on life. For no particular reason, I felt a little bit more optimistic. My attitude at work began to change, and I got myself back on track.

I share this story not to tout the benefits of steady exercise—which I highly recommend—but to illustrate the point that the activities required to obtain balance in your life may not be obvious to you at first. In fact, they may be the opposite of what you think you need. In my case, in order to cure my fatigue, I needed to expend energy, not conserve it.

Many other aspects of balance behave the same way. For example, if you feel tired, you may not need sleep but you may actually need to go run for a few miles. If you are feeling like you need to focus more on yourself, you may actually need to help someone else out besides yourself. If you are feeling hungry, you may need to eat healthier in order to regain your focus. If you are feeling like you can't meet deadlines unless you speed up, perhaps you need to take a step back and slow down for a while so you can see where you need to go faster.

Chapter Summary

- Today, we are more productive than ever, but we work even harder.
- Workaholism is rampant in today's corporate world, and technology isn't helping.
- People are motivated to overwork for the following reasons:
    - Personal gains
    - Survival
    - Self-worth
    - Passion
- There are three fake solutions to achieving work-life balance. Recognizing them for what they are is the first step toward getting back into balance:
    - Multitasking
    - Working harder
    - Giving it three more years
- Achieving balance is your responsibility, not your employer's.
- To achieve work-life balance, ask yourself three critical questions:
    - 1) What are your deepest values?
    - 2) How much time do you allocate to those values?
    - 3) What actions, if taken, would help you live closer to your values?
- Use the following executional tips when times get tough:
- Learn to say "no."
    - Keep commitments to yourself first.
    - Figure out what works for you.

FINAL THOUGHT: GO THE DISTANCE

I N 1976, THE OSCAR WENT TO *ROCKY*, THE ICONIC FILM ABOUT A mediocre boxer with a huge heart, who is given the chance to fight the heavyweight champion of the world, Apollo Creed. Apollo is known for his superior physicality, unbelievable speed, and self-aggrandizing showmanship. Rocky is awkward, slow, and scrappy, but has an iron will and a jaw of steel. The film follows Rocky along his journey to overcome self-doubt and train for the fight of his life. In what I consider to be the thematic monologue of the movie, Rocky explains his definition of success to his girlfriend, Adrianne, the night before the fight:

"It really don't matter if I lose this fight. It really don't matter if this guy opens my head either. 'Cuz all I wanna do is go the distance. Nobody's ever gone the distance with Creed. And if I can go that distance, and seeing that bell ring and I'm still standing, I'm going to know for the first time in my life, you see, that I weren't just another bum from the neighborhood."

In case you don't understand "Rocky speak," Rocky's interpretation of success is to make it to the end of the last round without having been knocked out by Apollo. His is not a mindset of glory or showmanship. He doesn't want fame or fanfare. He simply wants to take as many punches as Apollo throws at him without going down.

Apollo has an entirely different definition of success. He is a fighter who wants to win by the glorious "KO." His desire is to show everyone that he could easily beat Rocky but is mercifully willing to let him put up a fight for a couple of rounds. In the end, the fight goes all fifteen rounds, and Rocky loses by decision to Apollo. It's a personal victory for Rocky! Yet for Apollo, making it through to the end only to win by decision wasn't good enough. And thank goodness for that—otherwise, we wouldn't have *Rocky II*!

Think about how differently Rocky and Apollo would approach corporate life. Here are a few ways their two mindsets would manifest themselves at work:

Apollo: Get to the top as fast as I can without regard for others. Promotion trumps relationships. *Rocky:* Build experience and relationships along the way; get promoted when I'm ready.

Apollo: I am smarter than my boss; I should have his job. *Rocky:* Regardless of how smart I am, I know that I can learn a lot from my boss to make me better at my craft.

Apollo: I need to look good in front of others to get promoted. *Rocky:* I need to become valuable by being helpful to others so they'll want me on their team.

Apollo: I need to crush my opponents so they are not a threat to me. *Rocky:* I need to prove to myself that I can be successful. If others are successful too then that's fine by me.

Apollo: I will sprint to the finish line. *Rocky:* I will pace myself and prepare for a marathon.

My money is on the Rocky Balboas of the world. I believe that a long, prosperous career is not about getting riches or glory early on. A career is not a one- or two-round fight that ends in a knockout; it is a thirty-year slugfest of hard work, ups and downs, good times, and bad times. You are likely to have great successes and wins over the years, but you will also likely take some blows. The key is to keep getting up when others are staying down. Those who are willing to go the distance are those who will ultimately win the corporate fight. So take these corporate skills and use them. Enjoy the ride in front of you!

Made in the USA
Middletown, DE
24 June 2022